The Real and Assumed Personalities of Famous Men: Rafael De Nogales, T. E. Lawrence, and the Birth of the Modern Era, 1914 - 1937

Kim McQuaid

Gomidas Institute
London

FUNDAÇÃO
CALOUSTE
GULBENKIAN

This publication has been made possible with the generous support of the Calouste Gulbenkian Foundation.

Photocredits:
Reprinted with permission. The Imperial War Museum for photographs of T. E. Lawrence Q59314 and Q59314A; New York Public Library for portrait of Muna Lee and portrait of Constance L. Skinner; National Library of Scotland for R. B. Cunninghame Graham photograph; Audiovisual Archives, National Library of Venezuela, for Gen. Elezear Lopez Contreras and for Juan Vicente Gomez images. Photographs also scanned from Rafael de Nogales, *Four Years Beneath the Crescent* (London: Sterndale Classics) and *Memoirs of a Soldier of Fortune* (London: Wright and Brown).

Published by Taderon Press by special arrangement with the Gomidas Institute.

ISBN 978-1-903656-97-6

Gomidas Institute
42 Blythe Rd.
London, W14 0HA
United Kingdom
Email: *info@gomidas.org*
Web: *www.gomidas.org*

For Mirela Quero de Trinca

*. . . a Venezuelan historian who recognized the importance
of their countryman;*

*And for Dan H. Fenn, Jr., of Lexington, Massachusetts, the Kennedy White
House, and the Kennedy School of Government at Harvard University,*

. . . an honest person, a good friend, and a fine man to have in a musket fight.

TABLE OF CONTENTS

Illustrations

SUMMARY

T. E. Lawrence (1888-1935) and Rafael De Nogales (1879-1937) had careers which intersected and clarified many of the major attributes of the modern era. These include the rise of cheap energy, the oil age and global petroleum companies; the birth of the modern "Middle East"; the rise of religion as a political marker in emerging societies; and the slow decline of British imperial ascendancy and the gradual rise of the "dollar diplomacy" and increasingly global military activities of the U.S.A. Other key changes were heightened concerns about "crimes against humanity" involving massacres, ethnic cleansing and genocide and the increasing use of electronic media like radio and films as political mobilization machines and propaganda and persuasion tools. "Lawrence of Arabia" was one of the most famous figures to emerge from World War I. His Venezuelan contemporary, Rafael De Nogales, remains almost completely unknown outside of his native country. One fought with the Arabs against the Turks; the other fought with the Turks against Arabs, Armenians, Australians, British and Russian forces. Comparing and contrasting the careers of the two men helps clarify differences and similarities in historical narrative and analysis of a formative period of world affairs.[*]

---

[*] The "real or assumed personalities" phrase comes from the English translation of Falih Rifki Atay's *The Ataturk I Knew* (an abridgement of his *Cankaya*) (Istanbul, Isis, 1981) p. 9; This essay benefits from translations from the Turkish by Halit Akarca., then a graduate student at Princeton University and from the Spanish by James V. Pavlish of Lake Erie College.

RAFAEL DE NOGALES AND LAWRENCE OF ARABIA DURING WWI

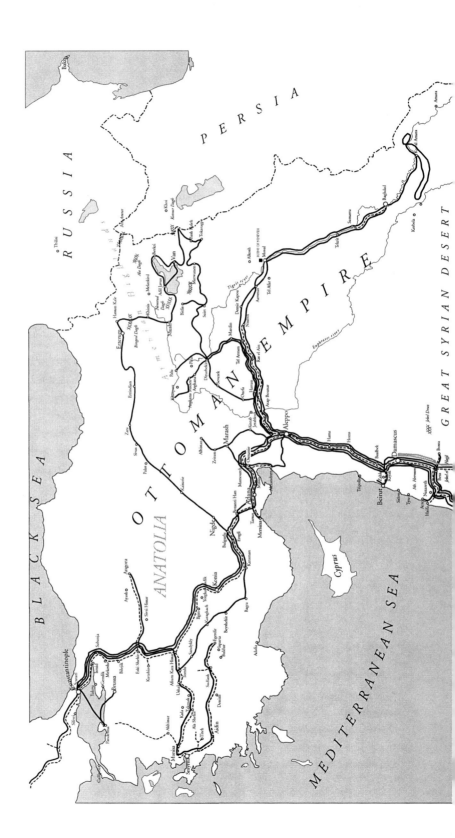

KEY

Rafael Nogales = 1915 - 1918

Lawrence of Arabia = 1916 - 1918

Railroads

Canals

EGYPT

SUDAN

RED SEA

ARABIAN DESERT

Medina

Jidda

Yenbo

Rabegh

El Ula

Hedia

Medan Salih

Tebuk

Wish

Abu Raga

El Kurr

Hallat Amar

Mudowwara

Maan

Akaba

Kossaima

Nekhl

Magdaban

Djebel Maghara

Port Said

Suez

Cairo

Alexandria

Jerusalem

Jaffa

Hebron

Jericho

Nablus

Es Salt

Amman

Nebk

Ghana

Neamiya

Abu Aus

Disad

El Kerak

Dana

Ellim

Mazar

Tyre

Beirut

Banat

Chapter One

Men of War and Letters

In late 1926 and early 1927, two memoirs of war in then-rarely-visited lands appeared with major commercial publishers in New York: Rafael De Nogales' *Four Years Beneath the Crescent* and Thomas Edward Lawrence's *Revolt in the Desert*. Both books chronicled the fall of the Ottoman Empire and the uncertain and fragile birth of the modern "Middle East". Both books were authored by gentleman officers who used autobiography as a narrative with which to address key issues of religion, ethnicity, and nationalism. Both authors wrote frankly, and with blood on their hands. Both had used their impressive linguistic facility to serve with and help lead Arabic and Turkish-speaking military units throughout their military service. Neither was rich in flattery for allies or opponents. Both were sardonic romantics and cultural outsider "loners" who presented individual will and personal heroism as an antidote to the mass-produced slaughter of the bloody and indecisive trench warfare that composed so much of World War I. Both wrote movingly about subsidiary battle-fronts where the industrialization of conflict was less thorough, barbed wire and machine guns were rare, and where successful cavalry (or camel) charges could still be made. War was, accordingly, still an occasion for chivalrous gentlemen and noble virtues. The grim existentialist realism of veterans like Eric Maria Remarque's *All Quiet on the Western Front*, Robert Graves' *Goodbye To All That*, Richard Aldington's *Death of a Hero* and Ernest Hemingway's *A Farewell To Arms* were still two or three years away from publication.[1]

---

1 Rafael De Nogales, *Four Years Beneath the Crescent* (New York, Scribner's, 1926; T. E. Lawrence, *Revolt in the Desert* (New York, George H. Doran, 1927). Eric Maria Remarque's and Robert Graves' books appeared in 1928; Aldington and Hemingway's in 1929.

Rafael De Nogales' *Four Years Beneath the Crescent* of 1926 chronicled the war service of a Venezuelan national who had fought with Ottoman army cavalry units in Anatolia, Mesopotamia, Syria-Palestine and in the Egyptian Sinai from 1915 to 1918, while rising to the rank of Major. T. E. Lawrence's *Revolt in the Desert* told the often-deemed heroic tale of an archaeologist who had helped create a Bedouin army which had raided and scouted for the British in their war against the Ottoman Turks and their German and Austro-Hungarian military advisers and allies on the Syrian, Arabian and Egyptian fronts from 1916 to 1918.[2]

Both "Lawrence of Arabia's" memoir and Rafael De Nogale's tale were well-crafted. Lawrence had rewritten his entire manuscript three times, with the occasional editorial aid of George Bernard Shaw, before publishing it privately in a one hundred copy subscriber's edition costing about one thousand of today's dollars per volume in 1921, and titled *Seven Pillars of Wisdom*. All of this was six years before his popular *Revolt in the Desert* abridgement appeared. Nogales, meanwhile, had destroyed eight earlier versions of his *Four Years* before getting a ninth attempt published in a 1924 Spanish edition and a 1925 German edition, prior to his 1926 English translation.[3]

Following their public appearance in England and the United States, both volumes were widely and well-reviewed. Lawrence's book, published several months after Nogales', was instantaneously

2   For a recent survey of the German and Austro-Hungarian military presence in the Middle East, see, Hans Werner Neulen, *Adler Und Halbmord: Das Deutsch-Turkische Bundis, 1914-1918* (originally titled: *Feldgrau in Jerusalem: Das Levantkorps des Kaiserlichen Deutschland)* (Frankfurt and Berlin, Ullstein, 1994).
3   Rafael De Nogales, *Cuatro Anos Bajo La Media Luna: Su Diario e Impresiones Durante La Guerra Mundial en los Diversos Frentes De Europa y Asia* (Madrid, Berlin, and Buenos Aires, Editora International, 1924); Rafael De Nogales, *Vier Jahre unter dem Halbmond: Erinnerungen aus dem Weltkriege: Autoriserte Deutsche Ausgabe* (Berlin, Reimar Hobbing, 1925.

anointed a literary classic, doing nothing whatsoever to decrease Lawrence's already widespread media celebrity in the United States.

Nogales, meanwhile, basked in a sea of lively compliments of his own. "Invaluable," "vivid objectivity", "engrossing", "the most thrilling adventure story to come out of the World War", "delightfully entertaining," "written with absolute candor," and a mix of "good prose" and "great adventuring," were phrases that appeared in reviews ranging from the conservative *New York Herald Tribune* to the liberal *Nation*. The *Times of London* joined the *New York Times* in welcoming the book; and the *New York Times'* reviewer of the English edition concluded that it "...would be worth its weight in thrills, if every page weighed a ton, as a tale of chivalry in an age of iron."[4]

Dissents from what most reviewers saw as Nogales' impartiality, sincerity, and knightly charisma were rare. The *Washington Post* did so by complimenting his "gifted and vivid pen dipped into a thousand colors to paint unforgettable vignettes" – before arguing he had whitewashed the Ottoman regular army of involvement in wartime atrocities.[5]

Selective Truths

In simple terms, Rafael De Nogales was Lawrence of Arabia in reverse. This meant more than the fact that Nogales had fought for the Turkish army against the British and their Arab guerilla allies. It

4   See, i.e., *Bookman*, Vol. 64 (September, 1926), p. 106; T. C. Martyn, "No Mercy East of the Hellespont," *New York Times Book Review* June 20, 1926, p. 18; *Times of London Literary Supplement*, June 17, 1926, P. 403; *Boston Transcript*, June 5, 1926, p. 5; *International Book Review*, July 26, 1926, p489; *New York World*, May 9, 1926, p. 6; *Nation*, Volume 123, (October 20, 1926), P. 408.

5   *The Washington Post*, August 1, 1926, p. S-12. In general, however, both Nogales and Lawrence came across as chivalric knights-errant, as gifted with the pen as they were with the sword. Both mens' portions of fame, however, came to them at a significant price. For they were not always who they said they were, and both told tales that were truer than the truth.

also meant that he was as publicly different from Lawrence as he was privately similar to him. Lawrence, for example, was intellectual, accomplished, well-networked with the English governing classes of his era and honored by significant numbers of his countrymen. Nogales was none of these things. Both, however, utilized a well-calculated medieval chivalry as a means of surviving in a sometimes very dangerous world.

Lawrence, the younger of the two men of war and letters, was born in 1888, the second of five sons in an Anglo-Irish landowning family. His father lived on remittances and was an enthusiastic hobbyist. His devout mother oversaw the education of a precocious Thomas and his brothers: first at high school in Oxford, and later at the university there. Thomas thrived in a world of books and ideas, and developed particular fluency in languages, literature, archaeology, and architecture. In 1910, aged 21, he put his undergraduate skills together to obtain a first class undergraduate degree in history, with a thesis on the architecture of Crusader military castles in Syria, Palestine, and southern Turkey. To gather material, Lawrence journeyed alone through all these regions, familiarizing himself with regional peoples and customs to unusual degrees. After his undergraduate work, Lawrence's Oxford mentor, D. G. Hogarth, Keeper of the Ashmolean Museum, got him a four year research scholarship, which Lawrence used to become part of a British Museum expedition excavating an important Hittite city near the current Turkish-Syrian border.

Toiling at excavation and perhaps amateur intelligence gathering and mapping work for Hogarth over the next four years, Lawrence was well positioned to become part of the British intelligence service office in Cairo once the Ottoman Empire entered World War I on the side of Germany and Austria-Hungary on November 1, 1914. In Cairo, Lawrence specialized in reports regarding the large Arabic-speaking portions of a Turkish-ruled realm. Lacking significant military training, Lawrence was nevertheless part of a very small and close circle of men with Oxford connections. Hogarth of the

Ashmolean, for example, has been called Lawrence's "substitute father" by several of Lawrence's biographers. When Hogarth arrived in Cairo early in 1916 to head the "Arab Bureau" of British intelligence, therefore, Lawrence's gentleman-officer career took a decided upswing.[6]

Reasons here had little to do with the Arabs and much to do with several major British military setbacks. First, there was a failed effort, early in 1915, to force the Dardanelles, occupy Constantinople and knock Turkey out of the war in one dramatic move. Sunken and disabled battleships, 265,000 Allied casualties (of which 46,000 were dead) and 8 ½ months later, the "Gallipoli" campaign's major success was a successful withdrawal of defeated Australian, British, and allied troops from pinched beachheads. As Gallipoli ended in January of 1916, another round of defeat was beginning. At Kut-el-Amara on the Tigris River in modern-day Iraq, a large Anglo-Indian effort to capture Baghdad went awry. Kut's surrender after a four month siege on April 29, 1916 marked one of the largest military defeats in British history, the worst in fact between the Battle of Yorktown in 1781 and the surrender of Singapore to the Japanese in 1942. Casualties at Kut totaled 23,000, of which 13,000 were marched into captivity. Twice in five months, Turkish forces had handed the British stunning military reverses. Bloody stalemate, meanwhile, continued in Flanders (where two of Lawrence's younger brothers had already died in action); and, in March of 1916, a German-backed revolt shook Ireland in the Easter Rising.[7]

After stunning failures at Kut-el-Amara and Gallipoli, British leaders finally began getting serious about supporting an "Arab Rebellion" against Turkish authority led by the Shariff of Mecca, Islam's holiest city. Talks with the Shariff and his sons got underway

---

6 The literature on Lawrence is vast and will only be selectively cited here. For Hogarth's importance to Lawrence, see, i.e., Desmond Stewart, *T. E. Lawrence: A New Biography* (New York, Harper, 1977), p. 38; Phillip Knightly and Colin Simpson, *The Secret Lives of Lawrence of Arabia* (New York, McGraw-Hill, 1969, pp. 24-28.

in July, 1915 (as Gallipoli started to go wrong) and were finalized in January of 1916 (as the first effort to relieve Kut-el-Amara got badly mauled). The Shariff played along at being an Ottoman ally from February to June of 1916, and then declared war against Turkish authority on June 27th, two months after the Kut-el-Amara defeat, and six months after the failure at Gallipoli.

Once Bedouin-led campaigns against Turkish troops in and around the Arabian Peninsula began, liaison and intelligence officers were necessary to insure supplies, money, tactics, strategy, and hosts of political and religious considerations were all well-enough understood and agreed to by Arab and Briton alike to make cooperation possible. This meant finding young men – and one woman, Gertrude Bell – who were healthy, bright, ambitious, fluent (or fluent-enough) in Arabic and its various regional dialects, and experienced in the society and folkways of the portion of the Muslim world ranging from Yemen in the South to Syria in the North. There were not many of these people, inside or outside of the British army, especially because the Arabian Peninsula was still a land where non-Muslims were not normally allowed to travel or live.

Here was Lawrence's chance, and he took it. Exchanging a desk in Cairo for the back of a camel in October, 1916, Lawrence became a

---

7   Robert Rhodes James, *Gallipoli* (New York, Macmillan, 1965); Michael Hickey, *Gallipoli* (London, John Murray, 1995). The approaching 100th anniversary of the battle is finally getting Australian academics, in particular, interested in opening and using the Turkish archives of the campaign, effectively un-researched until now. For the status of the effort, see: Harvey Broadbent, "Completing the Story of the Gallipoli Campaign: Researching Turkish Archives for a More Comprehensive History," *Journal of the Society for Army Historical Research*, Vol. 85, (Autumn, 2007) pp. 208-23. Kut-el-Amara has very rarely been written about, in proportion to its importance. See, for a rare exception. Ronald Millar, *Death of an Army; the Siege of Kut, 1915-1916* (Boston, Houghton Mifflin, 1970). For participant accounts, see: E. W. C. Sandes, *In Kut and Captivity With the Second Indian Division*, (London, John Murray, 1919) and Aubrey Herbert, *Mons, Anzac and Kut* (London, Arnold, 1919).

liaison and political intelligence officer – one who used his opportunity of contact and liaison with the Shariff of Mecca's sons very ambitiously indeed.[8]

T. E. Lawrence

As Lieutenant T. E. Lawrence started his mythic and real transformation into Lieutenant Colonel "Lawrence of Arabia," a very different man had entered his second year as a staff, logistics, and cavalry officer in the regular Ottoman Army. Rafael De Nogales was 10 years older than Lawrence, but he had done much less with his educational and career opportunities; in part this was a question of position. Lawrence, for example, operated at a vital center of global power, and as a supporter of an empire then controlling one-fifth of Earth's land area. Rafael de Nogales of San Cristobal, Venezuela was from what was then the global periphery, a non-affluent American republic with a long heritage of military rule and violent coups. As Britain was the possessor of an empire "on which the sun never set," so Venezuela

---

8   Two of Lawrence's early admiring biographers were poet novelist Robert Graves *Lawrence and the Arabian Adventure* (New York, Doubleday Doran, 1928) and military reformer and historian Basil Henri Liddell Hart (*Lawrence of Arabia* (New York, Blue Ribbon Books & Halcyon House, 1935 and 1937). For their queries to him and his answers re: his early activity, see: T. E. Lawrence, *T. E. Lawrence To His Biographers Robert Graves and Liddell Hart* (London, Cassell, 1963 and Westport, Connecticut, Greenwood, 1976).

was a country that neighboring Latin Americans described as an "armed camp."[9]

Nogales and Lawrence shared one essential characteristic, however, that explained much about both men's careers. Their silence about their families was close to absolute. Lawrence's family secret was illegitimacy. His father, an Anglo-Irish baronet, had abandoned his wife and four daughters on an estate in Ireland and started a new life, with a new name, at age 40, with a servant with whom he had fallen deeply in love. The five sons of the new union were raised in a strict evangelical home of unremarkable opinions and traditional loyalties to God, sovereign, and empire. Bastardy, however, helped insure that very few got close to the Lawrence family or children.[10]

Nogales' secret was probably similar. Two birth dates – 1877 and 1879 – exist for Rafael, the only son of Colonel Pedro Felipe Inchauspe Cordero and Maria Josefa Mendez Brito, a well-to-do couple of Spanish (Basque) and Native American descent. One of October 14, 1877 is recorded by Nogales' premier Venezuelan biographer; the other, two years afterwards, was repeatedly recorded by Nogales himself. Rafael was sent to boarding school in Germany and Belgium at age seven or eight, assuming the most commonly

9 For a concise and clear introduction to Venezuelan history, see, for example, Daniel Hellinger, *Venezuela: Tarnished Democracy* (Boulder, Colorado, Westview Press, 1990.

10 Lawrence's illegitimacy was not ever mentioned in print in his lifetime. A French book by Leon Boussard, *Le Secret du Colonel Lawrence*, first noted the fact in 1941. Lawrence's friend Ronald Storrs wrote a very diplomatic version of the truth in English in *The Dictionary of National Biography – Supplement, 1931-1940* (Oxford, Oxford University Press, 1949), p. 528. A huge dispute, however, occurred in Britain – and, to a lesser extent, America – when Richard Aldington's *Lawrence of Arabia: A Biographical Inquiry* (London, Collins, 1955) mentioned this and other aspects of Lawrence's life. For this ugly episode in literary suppression and self-censorship, see: Fred D. Crawford, *Richard Aldington and Lawrence of Arabia: A Cautionary Tale*, (Carbondale, Southern Illinois University Press, 1998).

accepted birth date. There he stayed until his father died when he was eleven years old. At some indeterminate point either before or after her husband's death in 1890, Rafael's mother relocated to Spain, where she lived until she died in 1894, when Rafael was 16. Very shortly after his mother's death, Rafael, who had never returned to Venezuela, then did something highly unusual for any natural born only-son in any Latin American family of his time (or our own). When he was in Spain, presumably with his mother, he discarded his father's name and called himself Nogales, adding thereto the family name of his mother, Mendez. The Basque term "Inchauspe" means walnut or walnut trees, so does the Spanish term Nogales. But for a male heir to remove his father's surname in its original language raised as many eyebrows as would be raised today if a man named Eisenberg in German renamed himself Iron Mountain in English or one named Fitzgerald in Gaelic anglicized himself into Bastard of Gerald. In addition, to continue to carry the mother's surname for the rest of his life and regularly use it (Nogales Mendez, Nogales y Mendez, "Kid Mendez") clearly demonstrated higher degrees of maternal respect and attachment than paternal. It also ran a very strong risk – then and now in Latin America – of being perceived as *a hijo natural* (illegitimate child) or a *recogido* son of some other less important family (i.e. of a servant adopted or accepted into a more important family and raised as one of its own), as opposed to a *hijo varon* (legitimate male heir of a family's name and honor.)[11]

At the least, Nogales' curious actions seem to be those of an only son without normal amounts of respect or regard for his father. Recogido (or adopted) status could help explain this. Nogales was of the Inchauspe family, but perhaps he was not. Affluent and aristocratic, he was also uneasy and marginal. Once both his father and his mother were dead by the time he was 16, he was also, except for two sisters in boarding school in Belgium, even more on his own in life.[12]

Nogales, on his own in his twenties and thirties, made far less of his early circumstances than did a younger Lawrence, cosseted in academic circumstances at Oxford. Nogales studied in a military academy, travelled the world, and had other adventures including working as a cowboy along the Rio Grande, as a surveyor in Alaska, and as a silver-mine claim salesman in Nevada. For 20 years after his mother's death, he may also have lived on his portion of a significant parental estate.

Specifics of exactly what Nogales did, as we shall see, remain only partly known. Often, the line between where reality ends and invention begins is ambiguous. What we know for certain is that Nogales, after brief stays in Venezuela in 1901 and 1908-1911, returned abroad and worked against the regimes of two successive Venezuelan dictators, Cipriano Castro (1899-1908) and Juan

11   For the differing birthdates, see: Dr. Kaldone G. Nweihed, *The World of Venezuelan Nogales Bey/Venezuelali Nogales Bey'in Dunyasi* (Ankara, Venezuelan Embassy, 2005) pp. 9, 23; Percy A. Martin (ed.) *Who's Who in Latin America: A biographical Dictionary of Outstanding Living Men and Women…* (Stanford, California, Stanford University Press, 1935), p. 279; for the name change, see: "Mendez 'Talks Much and is Annoying on that Account,' says [Jose M., ('El Mocho') Herandez," *New York Herald* August 5, 1913, page 10. This paragraph benefits from conversations with Mirela Quero de Trinca, author of *Rafael De Nogales Mendez, 1879-1937* in the *Biblioteca Biografica Venezolana* series (Caracas, Venezuela, C.A. Editora El Nacional, August, 2005).
De Trinca notes that Rafael De Nogales dealt with another case of a person claiming to be an illegitimate son fathered by, but not legally recognized by Colonel Inchauspe in the 1920's on behalf of the family. (De Trinca(2005), pp. 81-82).
Dr. Kaldone Nweihed is the pioneering analyst of Nogales' life. His work on gathering materials and confirming stories required intense dedication over a period of approximately 15 years.
12 Aristocratic women were exceedingly constrained in Venezuela, while aristocratic men were not. Mistresses abounded, and so many unions were not legitimized by civil or religious ceremonies that over half of all births in Venezeula were illegitimate as late as the 1940's. See: Judith Ewell, "Ligia Parra John: The Blonde With the Revolver," in : William H. Beezley and Judith Ewell, *The Human Tradition in Latin America*. (Wilmington, Scholarly Resources, 1987) pp. 151-66.

Vicente Gomez (1908-1935). Mounting small border raids from his native Tachira state on the Venezuelan-Colombian border in September and October of 1911 and again in early 1914, Nogales presented himself as a supporter of Andean regional rights against a corrupt cabal in Caracas, the nation's capital. His first raid began with five men, and his second, with 16 men. Nogales was not good at cooperating with other rebel leaders, at home or abroad; and, accordingly, his small raids sparked off no wider uprisings. Sparks, as he later said, fell on damp wood.[13]

How uncooperative Nogales could be with fellow Venezuelan rebels was demonstrated in July and August of 1913, when he made his first appearance in U.S. papers including the *New York Times*, the *Chicago Tribune*, and the *Boston Globe*. Venezuelan politics was again unsettled. Cipriano Castro had been overthrown by Juan Vicente Gomez, his number two man and army commander, when he had gone abroad for medical care in 1908. From exile in Europe, Castro repeatedly sought to invade Venezuela and overthrow Gomez. In 1909, Castro, en route via passenger liner, was intercepted by a cooperative effort of the French, Dutch, British and American navies and intelligence services. In 1911, a second attempt misfired. In 1913, U.S. newspapers were full of news of yet-another Castro coup attempt.[14]

As the *New York Herald* and other papers headlined the sound and fury of invasion reports and marching armies, Nogales wrote a long

13 Amalia Lluch Velez, *Luis Munoz Marin: poesia, periodismo y revolucion, 1915-1930,* (San Juan Puerto Rico, Fundacion Luis Munoz Marin & Universidad del Sagrado Corazon, 1999), chapter 8, pp. 219 ff. covers Nogales' 1911 raid. A participant remembered it began with only 5 men. About his 1914 raid with 16 men, Nogales later wrote: "I thought of my little troop as a torch vainly trying to set fire to a forest of green wood." Nogales, *Memoirs of a Soldier of Fortune* (New York, Harrison Smith, 1931), p. 242.

14 For Castro's coup efforts, see: J. Fred Rippy and Clyde E. Hewitt, "Cipriano Castro, "Man Without a Country," *American Historical Review* Vol. 55 (October, 1949), pp. 36-53.

analysis of the Castro and Gomez regimes that dramatically wished a plague on both their houses. Both Castro and Gomez had created centralized systems of "polite thievery." Both dictators ran Venezuela as if it were their personal hacienda, using a despotic and efficient system of informers, spies, torturers and assassins to do it. Both were the creations of an "Invisible Government" in Caracas that made and un-made regional warlords who aspired to be national leaders. Both, however, might battle each other to death or debility. Then an all-inclusive Nationalist third force could enter the field, take over the reins of power, begin reforms, hold clean elections and create a genuine Republic, instead of a disguised dictatorship.[15]

No less than seventy percent of Venezuela's people would rally to the Nationalist Party if it had the right leadership, Nogales-Mendez claimed. The best-known Nationalist leader was General Jose Manuel Hernandez, nicknamed "El Mocho", a strongly nationalist *caudillo* (regional warlord) who had long opposed both Castro and Gomez. He, in Nogales' less-than-diplomatic estimation, was part of the problem, not part of the solution. Hernandez lacked competence, aggressiveness, and "force of character." He had, in fact, "none of the qualifications of a real leader." Younger blood and newer ideas from a newer generation were required.[16]

Given that General Hernandez was also the pioneering founder and creator of the Nationalist party, Nogales' verbal journalistic coup soon put him at the center of a generational brawl among émigré

15 Rafael de Nogales-Mendez, "Peace or War in Venezuela," *The South American* [bi-weekly, circa 1913-1921], July 15, 1913, pp. 117-18, 126-27; "[Nogales Mendez] Says That a Ring Rules Venezuela," *New York Times*, July 15, 1913, p. 5. For the contemporary press reports, see, i.e. *New York Herald*, August 5, 1913, p. 3; idem, August 6, 1913, p. 3.
16 As Venezuela had no national military academy until 1908 the rank of General was often a self-awarded honorific in this period. Successful caudillos like Castro and Gomez were also Generals. Nogales-Mendez, "Peace or War in Venezuela," *The South American* July 15, 1913, pp. 126-27.

Venezuelans. As headlines detailed both fictional and real moves against Castro and his supporters in Venezuela, General Hernandez returned from an unsuccessful lobbying effort in Washington, D.C. Some impatient self-styled "Young Turks" in the Nationalist organization expressed disappointment that Hernandez had sought U.S. governmental support at all; others complained he had not received it; still more grumbled they were not consulted by Hernandez. Publicly, on August 4th, "General" Rafael de Nogales-Mendez spoke for all those who thought that a 60-year-old Hernandez was too old to lead troops in the field yet again. Privately, he deplored Hernandez's effort to gain support from the "Yankees," and in a letter, he wrote to a friend and told him he was heading for his native Andean region to fight via the nearby Dutch island of Curacao.[17]

Hernandez, for his part, reacted angrily. He did not hesitate to term Nogales a "pinhead", a "self-styled" general and "practically unknown" in the Nationalist party. "'What he says has no more weight than the wing of an insect... But he talks much and he is annoying on that account,' growled El Mocho."[18]

By the time summaries of these press reports and Nogales' intercepted letter arrived in the hands of Juan Vicente Gomez's spymasters in Venezuela, Castro's apparent last and final invasion effort was over. A landing at Coro, on the Venezuelan coast approximately 150 kilometers south-southwest of Curacao was

---

17 "Revolution On Here Against 'El Mocho' [Hernandez's nickname]: 'Young Turks', as the New Party Calls Itself, Believes Ancient Leader No Longer Useful," *New York Herald*, August 4, 1913, p. 9; De Trinca (2005), op. cit., p. 44 (quoting Nogales in a letter to a friend in Curacao in the Dutch West Indies intercepted by Gomez's agents.

18 "Mendez Talks Much and Is Annoying on that Account, Says Hernandes." *New York Herald*, August 5, 1913, p. 10; For the "exceedingly limited" power of the Nationalists in Venezuela at the time, see "General Andrade says Castro is not near Coro", *New York Herald*, August 8, 1913, p. 10.

reported defeated as early as August 12th, with rebels in Nogales' native Tachira State also reported dispersed into neighboring Colombia. Thorough government-controlled press censorship then produced glowing official reports of more Gomez victories, including the capture of Castro's son and brother in-law, and empty promises by Gomez aimed at U.S. investors to "restore civil rule" in six months.[19]

Gomez's press exaggerations and political hypocrisies, ironically, were largely unnecessary. U.S. and European leaders generally had no desire whatsoever to restore the rule of dictator Cipriano Castro, a "stormy petrel" whose refusal to repay foreign loans had led to European naval interventions in Venezuelan ports in 1902 and 1903, and U.S. fears of the supposed sanctity of its "Monroe Doctrine". Juan Vicente Gomez's 1908 coup had enjoyed U.S., British, French and German support. This was especially true after Gomez began negotiating freer trade, more orderly debt repayment and easier access for foreign investment in emerging strategic industries such as petroleum only two days after seizing power. Gomez, unlike Castro, was a tyrant who paid his creditors, understood that foreign navies protected him from Castro's return and so did not make an international nuisance of himself. This played especially well with U.S. leaders who had enunciated a "Roosevelt Corollary to the Monroe Doctrine" in 1904 to underline American hegemony and police power in and around the Panama Canal (built from 1904 to 1914). So long as Gomez avoided "chronic wrongdoing" like international economic disputes or "impotence" like allowing chronic domestic political instability, U.S. diplomatic and military power would assist him against external threats to his regime.[20]

---

19 See *New York Herald*, August 9, 1913, p. 4, August 10, 1913, p. 3, August 12, 1913, p. 10, August 15, 1913, p. 9, August 19, 1913, p. 11, August 23, 1913, p. 9, and August 26, 1913, p. 11.

The national interests of greater powers, therefore, insured that a combined invasion of Venezuela from both the west and the east undertaken by General Hernandez and others—including Nogales— early in 1914 failed after authorities on the British Guiana-Venezuela border blocked Hernandez's passage into Venezuela. Nogales accordingly, again, raided briefly in the west along the Venezuelan-Colombian border regions and then retreated.[21]

20 For contemporary negative-reaction to Cipriano Castro, see, i.e., "Cipriano Castro. Venezuelan Outcast...", *New York Herald*, August 10, 1913, p. 3 and "All Latin America To Feel Iron hand of the U.S.: Castro Revolt May Force President to Take Immediate and Drastic Action," *Chicago Daily News*, August 2, 1913, p. 1. Brian Stuart McBeth, *Gunboats, Corruption, and Claims: Foreign Intervention in Venezuela, 1899-1908* (Westport, Connecticut, Greenwood Press, 2001) covers the claims. Lewis L. Gould, *The Presidency of Theodore Roosevelt* (Lawrence, Kansas, University Press of Kansas, 1991) covers "T. R.". A summary of the Roosevelt Corollary is in: Gearoid O. Tuathail, Simon Dalby, and Paul Routledge, *The Geopolitics Reader* (New York, Routledge, 1998), pp. 32-33; Dexter Perkins, *A History of the Monroe Doctrine* (Boston, Little Brown, 1963 (reprint of 1955 ed.)) is a good solid survey. David McCullough, *The Path Between the Seas: the Creation of the Panama Canal, 1870-1914* (New York, Simon and Schuster, 1977) covers Roosevelt's seizure of Panama.
21 Quero de Trinca (2005), pp. 43-44.

Chapter Two

Nogales Becomes a "Soldier of Fortune" to Gain Military Experience Abroad

After the miscarriage of his second "Garibaldean" effort to remake Venezuela via invasion from abroad in June of 1914, self-described "Young Turk" Rafael De Nogales was 35 years old. His prospects as political exile and would-be Venezuelan revolutionary were not good. Juan Vicente Gomez, patterning himself on Mexico's Porfirio Diaz (who ruled Mexico from 1876 to 1911 as an autocratic modernizer very friendly to foreign capital) was more strongly entrenched than ever. Abolishing the autonomy of regional power brokers, Gomez no longer had to play one caudillo off against another. Instead, he used oil monies to create a centralized state with himself at the head.

U.S., British, French, Dutch and other leaders all supported Gomez's regime. Privately, however, Gomez was personally distasteful to many policymakers in the State Department and the White House. In 1918 Woodrow Wilson, for example, exploded to his Secretary of State that Gomez was a "scoundrel" who "ought to be put out" because Gomez's autocracy included moral support for Germany in World War I. Gomez, however, was also deemed to be a necessary strong man in a violent and disorderly society. His techniques produced "medieval despotism" and "the worst days of the Inquisition," on occasion, regarding personal and civil liberties. But there was, U.S. diplomats believed, no better alternative to what Secretary of State Robert Lansing called in 1917 "severe and purely selfish" rule and a government by "terrorism".[22]

There were plenty of places, U.S. leaders reasoned, less peaceful than Gomez's Venezuela. Policing the Americas, besides, was bloody and complicated. U.S. Marines went into Nicaragua in 1909 and 1912, Haiti in 1914, the Dominican Republic in 1916, Cuba in

1917, Panama in 1918 and Honduras in 1919. Low-level border wars, meanwhile, occurred with Mexico from 1914 to 1916, punctuated by major battles at the Mexican port of Veracruz in 1914. So long as Gomez maintained order, U.S.-Venezuelan trade and commerce increased, and Gomez simply postured and did nothing to support the Kaiser outside of Venezuela; U.S. policymakers were going to do nothing to overthrow him. Gomez might be Venezuela's bastard, but he was not a threat to the United States.[23]

The outbreak of World War I in Europe in August, 1914 only further insured that Juan Vicente Gomez was likely to remain in power in Venezuela for the duration. War, however, quickly became a beckoning frontier for Rafael De Nogales. Though he had called himself a "General" as early as 1909, his actual combat leadership was limited to small cavalry raiding parties. If he wanted to get more significant military and battlefield experience, here was the chance of his lifetime. Given his age and lack of large-scale professional wars in Latin America, World War I was also probably his final chance. To Europe, accordingly, Nogales went. And, as young T. E. Lawrence marked time preparing maps waiting for a call to Military Intelligence at British military headquarters in Cairo, Rafael De Nogales sought to find an army interested in utilizing his services.

22 Michael L. Krenn, *U.S. Policy Toward Economic Nationalism in Latin America, 1917-1929* (Wilmington,, Delaware, Scholarly Resources, 1990) (esp. Chapter 6: "Everything But Democracy: Venezuela, 1917-1929", pp. 99-103).

23 For a readable and personalized treatment of the wars and occupations in Latin America after 1909, see: Hans Schmidt, *Maverick Marine: General Smedley D. Butler and the Contradictions of American Military History* (Lexington, University Press of Kentucky, 1987), esp. 38ff; See also: Lowell Thomas *Old Gimlet Eye: Adventures of Smedley Bulter* (New York, Farrar and Rineheart, 1933 and reprinted by the Marine Corps Association, Heritage Library, Quantico, Virginia, 1981). For Nogales' "Young Turk" self-description see: "Third Party in Venezuela; 'Young Turks will Try to Wrest Government From Both President Gomez and Gen. Castro", *Boston Globe*, August 8, 1913, p. 5.

Lawrence got his call to Cairo far quicker than Nogales found a military recruiter. Nogales, in fact, ended up "prey to the liveliest disillusionment." The chief problem was that he did not wish to give up his Venezuelan citizenship, and instead wanted to serve as a foreign officer, on his word of honor. The French offered him the French Foreign Legion (where French nationals alone were officers). The Belgians and others also required citizenship to be an officer in their forces. Not until he got to Bulgaria did things start moving Nogales' way.[24]

At the Turkish embassy in Sofia in January of 1915, however, Nogales finally met two men very interested in his services. The first,

Rafael de Nogales in Turkish uniform.

Turkish ambassador, politician and military officer Ali Fethi Okyar, was a prominent member of the Young Turks who had taken control of the Ottoman Empire in 1908. The second, a German military attaché named only "Major von der Goltz," may well have been a kinsman of Wilhelm Leopold Colmar von der Goltz, a 70 year old retired Field Marshal in both the German and the Ottoman armies whose experience in the Turkish empire went back to the 1880s, and who had just arrived in Constantinople to augment a German

---

24 Rafael De Nogales, *Four Years Beneath the Crescent* (London and New York, Scribner's, 1926, pp. 1-11). For scholarly convenience, this and all subsequent citations will be given to the reprint of Nogales' first book, published in London by Sterndale Classics in 2003. The page numbers to the 2003 edition are: pp. 6-16; esp. 13, 15.

Military Mission led by General Otto Liman Von Sanders, which had begun reforming portions of the Ottoman military in 1913.[25]

Both German and Turkish military reformers, simply, needed all the help they could get early in 1915. In the 30-and-more years that top-ranking Young Turks like War Minister and Acting Commander-in-Chief Ismail Enver had been alive, the Ottoman Empire had lost huge chunks of territory to (in order): Russia (today's eastern Turkey and Armenia), Britain (Egypt, Sudan, and, later, Cyprus), France (Tunisia), the Austro-Hungarian Empire (Bosnia-Herzegovina), Italy (Libya),

Enver Pasha

Serbia, Bulgaria, Montenegro, and Greece (most of the European holdings of the Empire in the Balkans, including Macedonia, Kosovo, and western Thrace). The last six Christian powers had all attacked the Ottomans in the first six years the Young Turks were in power from 1908 to 1914. Losses in the Balkan war of 1912-1913 alone cost the Empire one-third of its remaining territory. Paranoia, as Henry Kissinger has noted, is the mistaken impression that people

---

25 The German edition of Nogales' book, *Vier Jahre unter dem Halbmond: Erinnerungen aus dem Weltkriege* (Berlin, Reimar Hobbing, 1925), p. 17, also has Major von der Goltz; Marshal von der Goltz's biography and writings are in German. For a biography, see: Hermann Teske, *Colmar Freiherr von der Goltz: Ein Kämpfer für den militärischen Fortschritt* (Berlin: Musterschmidt-Verlag, 1957); Field Marshal von der Goltz arrived in Constantinople December 12th; while Nogales left Sofia in early January.

out there are trying to get you. There was nothing paranoid at all about Turkish military concerns early in 1915. Military reform was even more on Enver's mind because he had just led his country into World War I on Germany and Austria-Hungary's side in October of 1914.[26]

As General Liman Van Sanders and others assisted "an enormous military reorganization and reconstruction effort," Enver, who as war minister had already survived two coup attempts, busily purged the ranks of the Ottoman officer corps of men whom he thought opposed to military reform (and his regime). In 1913-1914 he forcibly retired 1,300 high-ranking officers, as much as one-tenth of the total. So many senior men went that majors (instead of major generals) could command divisions and colonels (instead of lieutenant generals) could command corps. The middle ranks of the officer corps (i.e.: majors), already weakened by huge Balkan War losses, were weakened further by the political purges. The professional soldiers that remained faced gigantic logistics, supply and transportation challenges in an empire that was then about one-third the size of the United States, with only 1.5 percent of the railroad mileage and fighting a four-front war.[27]

Turkish forces, then, had a huge scarcity of operational mid-ranking field officers. Not least because of ambitious offensives Enver either had or wished to have mounted against the Russians and the

26 For Turkey's less-than-forthright path to war, see: Ulrich Trumpener, *Germany and the Ottoman Empire, 1914-1918* (Princeton, Princeton University Press, 1968); Henry Morgenthau, *Ambassador Morgenthau's Story* (Garden City, New York, Doubleday Page, 1918).
27 Lieutenant Colonel Edward J. Erickson has, thankfully, just written what the then Chief of the Turkish General Staff has called the "first complete history of the Ottoman Army in World War One to be completed outside of Turkey.": *Ordered To Die: A History of the Ottoman Army in the First World War* (Greenwich, Connecticut, Greenwood, 2001). See esp. pp. xiii, 7, 9, 10, 12 (footnote), 16, 53, and 72 (footnote). See also, Liman von Sanders, *Five Years in Turkey* (1922) (Nashville, the Battery Press, 2000), for a more impatient and Prussian view.

British. Nogales' linguistic and cultural skills now got him a place in the Ottoman Army in a manner not dissimilar to the way that Lawrence's experiences got him a place in British Intelligence in Cairo from 1914 to 1916. Enver, fluent in German and a former Military Attaché in Germany, chatted with Nogales, also fluent in German, and from a German-educated Spanish-Indian-Venezuelan family. Enver regularly conducted personalized diplomacy and was prone to chivalric gestures. Later in the war, for example, he accepted the word of a captured Australian naval officer not to fight against Turkey again before releasing him so that he could marry the daughter of the British diplomatic representative to the Vatican. Nogales' word of honor to serve the Ottoman Army was, likewise, good enough for Enver Pasha. The same rules of personal oath-taking, after all, governed all the German officers then serving in Turkey in Turkish military units and formations. So Nogales, though from a neutral country (but with a pro-German dictator) was offered the same courtesy as his German counterparts. He was enrolled in the Ottoman regular Army as a cavalry captain with the support of the German Military Mission. Enver's chivalry complemented Ottoman military and diplomatic self-interest.[28]

A relieved Venezuelan, meanwhile, happily bought uniforms and outfitted himself; knowing he now possessed more official status than he had ever enjoyed anywhere on earth. Little did Nogales know, however, as he subsequently set-out on a difficult month-long,

---

28 Nogales, op. cit., p. 16; Morgenthau, op cit., pp. 258-60 (for the story of word of honor chivalry); Kaimakam and Major Hakki, *Hilal Altında Dört Sene ve Buna Ait Bir Cevap* (Istanbul, Askeri Matbaa,1931) preface.(with thanks to Mr. Halit Akarca, then of the graduate school of Princeton University, for this translation.)

Mehmet Necati Kutlu, *Türkiye'de Bir Gezgin Sövalye Nogales Mendez* (Istanbul, Gendas, A.S., 2000) is Nogales' more recent and updated Turkish biographer. His book was published in Spanish, as *Nogales Mendez: Un Caballero Andante En Turquia* by the Venezuelan Embassy in Turkey in 1998).

thousand kilometer journey to the Turkish Third Army in Eastern Anatolia, just how soon he would also be part of a "paradoxical survey of the hideous."[29]

29 Nogales, op. cit., p. 6.

Chapter Three

The Bloody Road to Van

The Ottoman Empire, early in 1915, was heading into a period of prolonged military and social crisis. Military defeat and invasions on three fronts caused removal of suspect Christian minorities in Anatolia and Thrace and along portions of the Ionian coast. In Eastern Anatolia, in particular, local removals turned into regional massacres and long death marches. What began as regional and selective operations cascaded into harsher and often-secretive national policies rationalized in terms of national salvation or religious war. A politics of the least common denominator ruled. In the east, local Turkish leaders expected widespread Armenian subversion and rebellion in cooperation with attacking Russian armies. Local Armenian leaders meanwhile expected selective or generalized slaughters of Armenians by Turks and Kurds, organized into gangs or local militia units. They also too-often presumed Russian support for Armenian independence that simply did not exist. In a low (or no) trust environment, zealots came to the fore, arguing that only preventive violence and collective punishments could preserve the lives of members of their groups. Ethnic cleansings and local religious wars took place in portions of an empire still trying to absorb hundreds of thousands of Muslims driven out of the Balkans by victorious Christian powers only several years previously. In a multisided struggle, the stronger killed the weaker; and the weaker, when they got a chance, killed those weaker still.[30]

Ottoman military vulnerability only exacerbated problems. As Nogales was en route to the fortress city of Erzurum in February and March of 1915, the Turkish Third Army had just lost half its numbers in a disastrous winter offensive against the Russians which Enver had ordered in December and January. A typhus epidemic subsequently killed many Turkish soldiers that Russian bullets had not, including a new commanding general. Crises now erupted elsewhere. On March 18, a large Franco-British fleet first tried to force the strait of the Dardanelles, directly threatening Constantinople on the Bosporus. Tension levels spiked and evacuations of government offices to the interior were planned. As Nogales volunteered for combat with a front line cavalry unit in April, a Russian summer offensive loomed in the east. British forces began an offensive against Baghdad up the Tigris and Euphrates Rivers and, on April 25th, the large scale British land invasion on the Gallipoli peninsula began – one aimed at taking Turkish forts in the rear and prying open the doors to the Ottoman capital. A sense of fighting with one's back to the wall produced hostile and aggressive responses.[31]

These responses came speedily in Eastern Anatolia. Starting in villages and small towns, Armenians were attacked and sometimes killed in connection with searches for weapons, deserters, or spies. When Armenians rebelled, fought back, or sought revenge, Turks or Kurds attacked, bled or fled. Counter-vengeance followed. Ascending spirals of violence drove many Armenians into larger towns. Nogales first heard anxious queries about the possibility of massacres from Armenian traders in Erzurum in March. He heard more rumors as he headed towards the Iranian frontier where his assigned unit was

---

30 The Armenian Massacres are exceedingly contentious and often discussed. Was it a consciously plotted genocide to destroy a people; an unnecessarily cruel and bloody removal that existed, in large part, because of Ottoman logistical and political disorganization; or a civil war within a portion of the Ottoman empire? For recent discussions of the major approaches, see, i.e., Taner Akcam, *A Shameful Act: The Armenian Genocide and the Question of Turkish Responsibility* (New York, Holt, 2006); Guenther Lewy, *The Armenian Massacres in Ottoman Turkey: A Disputed Genocide* (Salt Lake City, University of Utah, 2005); Justin McCarthy, *The Ottoman Peoples and the End of Empire* (London, Arnold, 1999).
31 Erickson, op, cit., pp. 54-60, 101, Robert Rhodes James, op. cit., pp. 39-97; Morgenthau, op. cit., pp. 184ff; Akcam, p. 126; Nogales, op. cit., pp. 47-48.

fighting. He had been a week en route when he saw his first mutilated Armenian bodies on the road on April 20th. The same day, he heard Armenians had rebelled in the nearby city of Van. He was about to discover Hell in some very small places.[32]

Who was attacking whom also quickly started to become unclear. In the fortress town of Adil Javus, Nogales was courteously fed, housed and greeted. The next day, April 21st, he awoke to gunfire and saw an attack on all the adult males in the Armenian quarter. Attempting to stop the killing, he was told by a local Turkish official that the governor-general of the province, Cevdet Bey, had ordered all Armenian males over the age of twelve put to death. "I, as a soldier," Nogales recorded, "could not prevent the execution of this decree, which was purely civil in character, however much I desired. So I ordered the gendarmes to retire, and waited until the hell was over." Subsequent efforts to save seven Armenian male survivors Nogales took prisoner also failed. The Armenians, a non-plussed Nogales was told, had attacked the town and been repulsed.

Moving on across a lake to a nearby village in a motor launch, Nogales luckily avoided Armenian irregulars, didn't comment on the mysterious disappearance, en route, of several Armenian sailors, and arrived in the midst of an unequal evening battle between Armenians and Kurds. Flames lifted themselves "like gigantic fiery serpents from among the ruins of a blazing church" as the military chief of the town gave Nogales a report and assigned him lodgings for the night. Peering out at the "gorgeous panorama of flames" surrounding him, shots rang out and a bullet passed through Nogales' coat-sleeve. The next morning, over a breakfast of welcome with several Kurdish Sheiks, Nogales watched Armenian positions taken from the rear, and all but two remaining Armenian adult males killed. Nogales' efforts to save these two by locking them up quickly failed. The wives and the children of the dead Armenians, meanwhile, were fed by the families of the same Kurdish tribesmen who had destroyed or driven

32 Nogales, op. cit., pp. 49-57.

Rafael de Nogales and his Kurdish bodyguard during the siege of Van.

away their husbands. "Barbarism hand-in-hand with charity" confused Nogales, even though draconian punishments in conflicts against guerillas are a norm whenever civilian populations will not identify the guerillas among them. For example, this was the case in the many "Indian Wars" in the U.S.A. Nogales, however, had not joined the Ottoman regular army to be a policeman or to engage in more Venezuelan border raids, but to fight European professional armies. His Turkish military service was off to an ironic start.[33]

Nogales' life soon got more paradoxical. It also became far busier and bloodier. Between April 14 and 20, a very uneasy standoff had existed between Governor-General (or Vali) Cevdet Bey and Armenian leaders in and around the city of Van. Rumors flew that a general massacre of all Armenians was planned for Sunday the 19th. A suspicious death of a top Armenian military leader on the evening of the 16th and the arrest and subsequent murder of the top Armenian political spokesman on the 17th worsened relations. As early as the 15th, the city of Van "looked like an armed camp." Cevdet, the son of a prominent local Turkish family, newly

33 ibid., pp. 58-62

appointed as Vali and with previous experience in the invaded border regions, appeared to see the best defense as being a good offense. He believed Russian-backed Armenian rebellion was inevitable. His status as a brother-in-law of Enver may also have reassured him about levels of support from Constantinople. Whatever his motives, Cevdet came down hard on dissent and potential dissent in a city which was an historic center of Armenian nationalism. In the process, he set an unfortunate precedent; one that was lethal for many inhabitants of Eastern Anatolia.[34]

Sunday the 19th came and went with mutual arms buildups, but no killings or shootings in Van. Armenians, instead, abandoned their homes on the outskirts of town and concentrated on fortified Armenian interior neighborhoods, especially those around a large American missionary compound and the German consulate. The consulate was permanently protected by the laws of nations. The extraterritoriality of the American mission was far less secure. The Young Turk regime had voided centuries-old "Capitulations" protecting foreigners from Turkish laws, taxes, and government when it allied with Germany and entered the First World War. The U.S.A, however, remained a neutral power (and never, in fact, declared war on the Ottoman Empire). Whether or not to attack the thousands of Armenians in and around the U.S. missionary compound, therefore, became a constant dispute between hard-liners including Cevdet and military men who believed they already had enough opponents

34 Two records of the day-to-day events in and around Van are: Clarence D. Ussher, *An American Physician in Turkey: A Narrative of Adventures in Peace and War (1919)* (London, Sterndale Classics 2002, esp. pp. 126ff.; Onnig Mekhitarian, "The Defense of Van," (Parts 1-4), *Armenian Review*, (Boston, Hairenik Association,. 1948), Volume 1, #s 1-4: pp. 121-29, 131-43,130-42, 133-42. Ussher was a physician and Congregationalist Missionary in Van; Mekhitarian was part of the Intelligence Agency within the "Military Council for the Defense of the Armenians of Van" established in April 18th. Recent Ottoman archives coverage of the Van events is Justin McCarthy, et. al. *The Armenian Rebellion at Van*, (Salt Lake City, University of Utah Press, 2007). See esp. pp 191-92.

without alienating the Americans (who were disarming Armenians who entered their compound, while, at the same time providing logistical assistance to armed Armenians outside the compound walls: a significant number of whom were members of their congregation).[35]

Facing the armed Armenians was a collection of Turkish forces that were mostly local militia units and untrained irregular Kurdish cavalry, leavened with a small number of regular army troops. On Monday the 20th, Turkish assaults on Armenian positions began. Initial efforts failed. When Nogales arrived on April 22nd, therefore, Cevdet promptly recruited him to operate old muzzle-loading fortress and field artillery; and, later, to lead offensives of comparatively well-trained gendarmes. In a coded dispatch dated April 23 or 24, Cevdet told his superiors that he had enrolled Nogales "for a few more days so he can fight against these insurgents", estimating their number at around 700 capable and well armed men.[36]

Nogales soon agreed with Cevdet's assessments. Skirmishes were bitter, resistance was stubborn, and prisoners were non-existent. "Nobody gave quarter or asked for it," Nogales wrote, "The Christian or Moor who fell into the enemy's hands was a dead man." By the 25th, both the city's cathedral and its ancient mosque were reduced to ruins on Nogales' orders after Armenians used them as snipers nests. Turkish forces besieging entrenched Armenians were also attacking outwards against Armenian rebels in outlying villages. No more than 60 miles behind these Armenian skirmishers was an invading Russian army fighting its way through mountain passes from the Iranian border. Justified fears of becoming the quarry, not the prey,

---

35 For specifics, see: Ussher, esp. pp. 147-51.
36 Deciphered telegram from Cevdet [Djevdet] Bey on 9/10 – 2 - 1331 April 23/24, 1915, published by the Archives of Military History of the Turkish General Staff in: *Askeri Tarih Belgeleri Dergisi* [The Journal of Military History Documents], Vol. 34, # 85 (October, 1985), pp. 40-41. Many thanks to Halit Akarca of Princeton University for this source and translation.

increasingly caused local Turkish militia and Kurdish Tribesmen to go home to protect their flocks and families. At the same time, Russian advances boosted the morale of the besieged Armenians. For three weeks, Nogales was part of a bitter and bloody military struggle fought mostly by irregulars on both sides.[37]

The often vividly bittersweet tales told by Nogales about this urban warfare avoid presenting either Turk or Armenian as always sinned-against and never sinning. Cevdet, for example, is presented as a gentlemanly, cultivated, bloody-handed scoundrel. But Armenian leaders come off little, if any, better. Very early in his memoir, Nogales criticized Armenian spokesmen for "immeasurable nationalistic ambition," said they had engaged in imprudent "star chasing," and claimed the Armenian massacres chiefly resulted from Armenians in eastern Anatolia seeking emancipation from Turkish rule, not autonomy or federalism within a Muslim-majority state. He argued the rebels in Van were well-armed with multi-shot Mauser machine pistols, were well organized, and were far more numerous than later Armenian (or even-later Turkish) histories relate. The events at Van in which Nogales participated were anything but chivalric or heroic; religious toleration did not exist; and accordingly, neither did mercy. "It is not the same thing," Nogales wrote, after describing Armenian riflemen targeting and killing an old Muslim woman hanging out clothes to dry on the roof of her home, "to read in newspapers about massacres, cruelty, and injustice, as to witness these things taking place on both sides, as I did on *many* occasions without being able to prevent them."[38]

Nogales' mix of empathy and distaste for both sides in what one side saw as a civil war on top of a foreign invasion and the other side saw as an intolerant and barbaric religious massacre put him in an unenviable position. He never argued that one side was entirely innocent and the other entirely guilty. Instead, both sides were guilty of different crimes: the Armenians of ill-considered rebellion; the

---

37 Nogales, op. cit., 68-83, quote on p. 68

Turks of ill-considered carnage. Neither side behaved chivalrously. Armenians, for instance, early on, tried to get some of Nogales' troops to mutiny by saying they should not obey the orders of a "Christian dog." On May 1st, Nogales' Muslim orderly told him that there were two Christian missionary nurses working in the Turkish military hospital and undergoing hardships. He went over to see if they were all right and got Cevdet involved in forcing improvements in their conditions. In return, an American nurse, Grace Knapp, later remembered him as a preening murderous liar with no respect for either Armenian or Turk.

The American nurse's memory of Nogales is worth quoting in full—if only to get an idea of just how rancid relations were between missionaries with Armenian congregations and Turkish officials in Anatolia at the time.

> During the siege we received a call or two from a man calling himself a German officer. As I remember him, he wore the uniform of a Turkish captain. He told us that he was a native of Venezuela, had been in Alaska and had been a cowboy on our own Western plains. He had also been to school in Germany and claimed to have a commission in the German army. One day he sent a note to Sister Martha, who immediately said, 'This settles it. He is not a German officer, for no man who writes German like this would ever receive a commission in our army.'
>
> From his own story we knew that he directed the bombardment of the walled city, but he acknowledged that it had not been a very successful piece of work.
>
> 'The cannon-balls go through the thick mud walls of the houses without destroying them, and the Armenians are grateful to us for

38 ibid. pp. 21, 22, 30, 45, 68, 85: for other Armenian massacres of Turkish civilians in Van immediately after a siege, see Ussher, op cit., esp. 154 and John Otis Barrows, *In The Land of Ararat, A Sketch in the Life of Mrs. Elizabeth Freeman Barrows Ussher* (New York, Fleming H. Revell, 1919), pp. 147-49. For a new volume using rarely-used Turkish archives, see *The Armenian Rebellion at Van* by Justin McCarthy, Esat Arslan, Camellian Taskiran, and Omer Turan (Salt Lake City, University of Utah Press, 2006), esp. 176-232.

having made another opening for them to shoot us through.' His contempt for the Turks was great, and we could not keep from laughing as he told how the men went about carrying explosives in their arms and lighted cigarettes in their mouths. Some of the awful wrecks of men we saw who had been blown up by their own cannon or ammunition proved that the common soldiers did not fully understand the nature of the materials with which they had to deal.

Captain de Nogales, as he called himself, was evidently a 'soldier of fortune,' adding to his already varied experiences by helping the Turks exterminate the Armenians. There was a large mirror in the room. At the close of each call the captain would bid us good-bye with a handshake and a low bow, then straighten up, click his heels in true German fashion, salute his own reflection in the mirror, turn, bow to us again and march out. His stay in Van was short, and then he was off in search of new adventures.[39]

Knapp's pen dripped bile about a man helping improve her conditions. Nogales' three weeks in Van, accordingly, did nothing for his repute in the United States. Much as he never bombarded the U.S. missionary compound, his Turkish officer status made him a barbarous enemy. Knapp, like most U.S. missionaries in Anatolia, was attracted to work with Armenians because conversions among them had been widespread. Until the oil age in the Middle East began for American multinational corporations twenty years later, religious school missions were the major U.S. presence in the entire region. Muslims, Jews, and Greeks within the Ottoman Empire almost never converted, while there were 40,000 Armenian converts living in the U.S.A. by 1914. In attacking Nogales, missionary Knapp was defending her congregation. So insistent was she about the task that she only reluctantly and partially recognized that many local Muslims around Van took women and girls into their [sic] "harem" [homes] to save them from massacre, before later leaving them with Christian

39 Grace H. Knapp. *The Tragedy of Bitlis* (1919) (London, Sterndale Classics, 2002), pp. 25-26. Nogales; op cit., pp 82-84.

missionaries when they fled Van in-advance of the Russian army in mid-1915.[40]

Nogales was not, however, the empty-headed adventurer Grace Knapp described. T. E. Lawrence later half ironically subtitled his memoir of World War I "A Triumph." Nogales' narrative was a more straightforward chronicle of survival against long odds. A Venezuelan political exile, we should understand, was very vulnerable. He did not even have his own diplomats or embassies to protect him. He was in the midst of an ethno-religious blood feud in a country also being invaded from three directions simultaneously. The German military mission in the Ottoman Empire was still very small. The nearest German officer was hundreds of miles away. Nogales had to adapt very quickly to his surroundings or die.[41]

He adapted, first by learning Turkish within his first six months, then by making and maintaining important friendships among fellow officers – both Turkish and German. Then, finally, he learned how to play German and Turkish military bureaucracies off against each other.

The process of bureaucratic infighting began in earnest once Nogales' division commander reclaimed his services from Cevdet on the 12th of May. As invading Russians fought through to Van in the next ten days, Nogales performed staff, logistics, and scouting duties

40 For the importance of missionaries, see: John De Novo, *American Interests and Policies in the Middle East, 1900-1939* (Minneapolis, University of Minnesota Press, 1963); pp. 8-9, 103; Knapp, *Tragedy of Bitlis*, p. 49. Missionary groups raised $100 million for Armenian Relief during and after World War I and the Massacres—a huge sum. See, i.e., Merrill D. Peterson, *"Starving Armenians": America and the Armenian Genocide, 1915-1930 and After*, (Charlottesville, University of Virginia Press, 2004), pp. 51 ff.
41 By early 1916, there were still only 290 German officers in the Ottoman Empire. Later that number rose—by 1917-1918—to 800 officers and 32,000 men. Isabel V. Hull, *Absolute Destruction: Military Culture and the Practices of War in Imperial Germany* (Ithaca, Cornell University Press, 2004), p. 269.

during a slow Turkish retreat. The skills of his immediate Turkish superiors impressed and reassured him. The commander of the Third Army, Lieutenant Colonel Halil Bey, however, emphatically did not. Personally brave, Halil was also, in Nogales' view, militarily incompetent. He handed off responsibility for his own failures to others and took credit for others' successes as his own. "His was only a stolen fame," Nogales wrote. As an uncle of Enver, he was also a "political general" who would do what was desired instead of what was militarily required.[42]

That also meant, Nogales strongly believed, that Halil enabled ongoing massacres undertaken by Cevdet for Halil's own non-military purposes. So, after another month in combat, Nogales requested to be relieved from his post as a provisional chief of staff of a well-trained gendarme regiment, among whom border guards, police, ex-bandits and guerillas were all numerous, and in which the standard punishment for insubordination was death. Once permission was granted, he prepared to return to headquarters for new orders.[43]

At this point, Nogales' unique position weighed heavily. He'd proven himself in bloody street fighting and cavalry attacks and defenses. Linguistic fluency and cultural accommodation was such that some fellow officers even began alerting Nogales to forthcoming massacres Cevdet was arranging. The killing of several thousand Armenian and Nestorian Christian males at Sairt, 100 miles west of Van, especially upset Nogales. Now revenge was getting out of hand, and he was starting to see too much.[44]

Timing, here, was important. By mid-June of 1915, killings and deportations had been variously underway in eastern Anatolia for a month. Cevdet alone had insufficient authority for such extensive activity. Gendarmes, normally national police under the authority of

---

42 Nogales, op. cit., pp. 94-95.
43 ibid., pp. 101, 108, 116.
44 ibid. pp. 108-09.

the Interior Ministry in Constantinople, were becoming involved in large scale local killings. At Sairt, the chief of the local gendarmes had even directed the massacre in person. Nogales, whose career included journalism, understood news like this was explosive, and that it was bound to leak-out.

Indeed, it already had. *The New York Times* ran its first story that massacres were happening on May 6. On May 24th, just after Nogales left Van, the British, Russian, and French governments issued an unusual joint declaration to the Ottoman government that they regarded persecutions and "mass murders" of Armenians as a "crime against humanity and civilization" for which they would hold "all members" of the Ottoman government and blameworthy subordinates *personally* responsible. Never before had a state's relations with its own citizens (as opposed, for instance, to one state's treatment of prisoners of war of another state) been diplomatically addressed in this fashion. Young Turk leaders responded – with the enthusiastic support of Germany's first wartime ambassador in Constantinople – they had a sovereign right of self defense against revolutionary movements aided by the Allies. London, Paris, and Petrograd, therefore, not the Young Turks, were responsible for whatever was happening in Armenian districts.[45]

Diplomatic thrust and parry about a new legal concept called "crimes against humanity" or suppressing large and dangerous revolutionary undergrounds was all very well. Nogales, however, was an Ottoman officer who had just commanded troops in the very city where the Armenian revolution had supposedly begun. He knew treason or loyalty in Anatolia was a patchwork quilt, not an either/or proposition; but he also increasingly thought Cevdet's killing was excessive. Men like him, he realized, could very easily pay the potential price for that. As a journalist, he also knew that fame could assist – and disgrace cripple – his future ability to reside in foreign

45 Ulrich Trumpener, *Germany and the Ottoman Empire 1914-1918* (Princeton, New Jersey, Princeton University Press, 1968) pp. 208-10.

lands like England or the United States. Lacking such tolerant havens from political oppression, longtime exile Nogales could be deported to Venezuela, there to face prison or a firing squad.[46]

There were many practical survival reasons, therefore, for Nogales to get as far away from Cevdet, Halil, and Anatolia as he could, and he did so. Later, charging murder plots against him by both Cevdet and General Halil also conveniently cast Nogales in a pro-Christian role. But Nogales, at this point in his military career, probably cared far more about his own life than theology – or the lives of either Armenians or Turks directly involved in what was often a brutal religious conflict.[47]

Nogales, therefore, simply left the "pageant of agony and blood" in Anatolia. Instead of heading north-northwest for Third Army headquarters in Erzurum however, he headed south-southwest for Aleppo in northern Syria. There, a different Turkish Army (the Fourth) and a different senior Young Turk leader (Cemal Pasha) were defending the Syrian-Arabian-Egyptian front semi-independently. In cooperation with a larger and more powerful German military mission than existed in the Caucasus border regions. Here, also, was a stubborn German consul, Walter Rössler, who opposed the removal or killing of Armenians; and a courageous Turkish governor, Celal (or Djelal) Bey, who strongly opposed Cevdet-like policies. Until relieved of their duties, both waged quiet but courageous struggles, with local Armenians and Muslims, to save many Armenians in the city and the orphans left behind by the dead and dying from other regions who

---

46 Cevdet, for example, supposedly allowed the killing of Armenian women and children in villages to begin on April 28th. Nogales also reports that Armenian guerillas and irregulars attached to the Russian army killed Muslim women and children on a regular basis, before and after this date. Nogales, op. cit., pp. 79, 89.

47 Here, I presume that ethnic-based nationalism primarily influenced a minority of educated intellectuals, and that religion primarily influenced the large majority of the uneducated and unschooled on both sides of the Christian/Muslim violence.

Turkish Dervish troops in field uniform.

transited through the city. In Syria, the patchwork of loyalties and actions that was the Ottoman Empire could operate in Nogales' favor. "I hoped," Nogales wrote, "to arrange for my discharge from the Ottoman army, or at least my transfer to another front."[48]

Nogales, at this point, was clearly playing a double game with his Third Army commanding general, Halil, whom he later called his "chief antagonist" in the Ottoman officer corps. The reason was that Nogales saw Halil as a political appointee who was Enver's uncle; just as Van governor Cevdet Bey was Enver's brother-in-law. "Political"

48 Nogales, op. cit., p. 119;- For specifics about Celal, and other high Turkish officials replaced or murdered for refusing to cooperate with Constantinople's anti-Armenian policies, see: Hilmar Kaiser, *At the Crossroads of der Zor: Death, Survival, and Humanitarian Resistence in Aleppo, 1915-1917*, (Princeton, Gomidas Institute, 2002), esp. pp. 14, 71; Taner Akcam, op. cit., pp. 166-68. M Rössler and Celal's efforts helped decrease the mortality among Armenians in Aleppo. See: Trumpener, op. cit., pp. 219, 227, 234. Aleppo was one of only three cities in today's Turkey and Syria where a full-scale deportation never happened. The other two being Istanbul and Izmir. See: Levy, op cit., pp 191ff.

officers like Halil, he believed, had "personal ambitions and political connections" that, in Michael Mann's words, "reinforced their defects of character" and made them willing to massacre Armenians, unlike the "professional soldiers" of the Turkish regular army, including Nogales. The extent to which only "political" men like Cevdet and Halil murdered Armenians and others or extorted money from them in Anatolia at this time is very debatable. What is not debatable is that Nogales feared Halil would murder *him*. Melodramatic or not, Nogales' fears led him to risk disobeying orders and being caught and tried for desertion.[49]

After disappearing and traveling south for weeks, however, Nogales reached Aleppo in mid-July. There, he got a "precious document" from a high ranking German military physician saying he needed "absolute rest" for several weeks for high fevers and dysentery picked up en route. Subsequently, the same physician said Nogales needed the attention of a medical specialist in Constantinople. Staying at a dormitory and club for German officers and engineers in Aleppo, Nogales probably told dramatic and tragic tales of his six months in the interior. He also found people he thought he could depend upon and even confide in. As opposed to feeling that a sword of Damocles was hanging over his head when speaking with men like a cultured governor of Dyarbekir who, Nogales claimed, prudently— as opposed to enthusiastically—obeyed orders from Constantinople regarding massacres; or avoiding speaking frankly with a military and gendarme commander in Diyarbekir who calculatedly exaggerated the numbers of military weapons seized from Armenian homes as local massacres continued.[50]

---

49 Nogales, op. cit., p. 92. Kaimakam and Major Hakki (1931) is the best source for Nogale's actions here. Michael Mann, *The Dark Side of Democracy: Explaining Ethnic Cleansing* (New York, Cambridge University Press, 2005), p. 263.

Rafael Nogales as Supply Officer in Palestine.

In addition to the German military mission – including the German chief of staff of the Ottoman Army back in Constantinople – Nogales also had the advantage of the personal support of Enver. In subsequent days, Nogales used both. His claims about who had given him what orders to go where were far less important than his desire to make himself symbolically high-profile enough that political animal Halil's ordering him back to the Third Army or punishing him would be contested and inconvenient. Major (Kaimakam) Hakki, a Third Army staff officer who was certainly no friend of Nogales, later recalled how Nogales' previous vocation of journalism "came in handy." German newspapers and the Turkish ones translating from them published long eulogies under the heading "'General Nogales' as soon as he arrived in Istanbul," Hakki wrote. Nogales, moreover, always kept these documents with him, "and whenever he was questioned about his identity he presented them."

50 Kaimakam and Major Hakki, op. cit., pp. 62-63; Nogales, Chapter 8, pp. 119 ff. Hans-Lukas Kieser says the Vali of Diarbekir "developed a particular zeal in the liquidation of Christian communities" in 1915-16. See his "Dr. Mehmed Reshid: A Political Doctor," in: Kieser and Schaller (eds.), *Der Volkermord und die Shoah*, Zurich, Chronos Verlag, (2002), 245-280, esp. 247.

With celebrity, Major Hakki and Nogales both knew, went protection.[51]

Enver, accordingly, seems to have married diplomacy and caution regarding someone he had, after all, *personally* enrolled in the Ottoman officer corps, and whose military identification documents he had himself signed. Refusing Nogales' request to leave the army, Enver approved further medical care and then assigned him to duties as a supply officer along a key portion of the primary transportation route to the Egyptian and the Mesopotamian fronts. Concern not to alienate his German ally, and, in particular, General Fritz Bronsart von Schellendorff, the "generous protector" and "excellent friend" of Nogales and chief of staff of the Ottoman Army, probably played the largest part in Enver's decision.[52]

---

51 Kaimakam Hakki (1931), p. 57.
52 Nogales, pp. 127, 137.

Chapter Four

Staying Alive

Once reassigned by War Minister Enver and Bronsart von Schellendorf, chief of staff of the Ottoman Army, in August of 1915, Nogales worked hard to improve efficiency and decrease corruption along a 100 kilometer/60 mile route in today's southern Turkey. If you imagine the Ottoman Empire of the time as a pair of scissors with Anatolia and points eastward to Constantinople as the head and Syria-Palestine-Arabia and then Iraq as its two long open blades, the Amanus Mountains and the nearby Taurus Mountains were the hinge around which everything turned. They were also the two crucial gaps in the railroad lines sometimes-fitfully connecting Constantinople with distant Ottoman battle fronts. As engineers dug five and six mile long tunnels through summits they could not build around, and since British and French fleets made Turkish seaborne transport along the eastern coast of the Mediterranean impossible, all the men and materiel heading for Turkish forces fighting from the Tigris and the Euphrates to the regions around Mecca and the Suez Canal moved, of necessity, along hurriedly constructed corridors where everything was trans-shipped via horse-drawn wagons, or the backs of camels or donkeys. Because supply failures regularly caused front-line Turkish regiments to lack basic items including shoes, ammunition, food, pay, and medical care, the logistics job involved here was not one for the squeamish.[53]

Nogales received free rein to improve matters from his immediate Turkish superiors, and what he called his "violent," "impatient" and "inflexible" character assisted his success. His job necessitated

---

53 For supply problems, see: von Sanders, Herbert, Erickson, and others. Erickson 2001 estimates that "first class infantry units typically would lose one-quarter of their strength to disease, inadequate rations, and poor hygiene while traveling through the empire." (p. 103).

simultaneously fighting bandits, jailing or exiling corrupt officers, whipping soldiers for stealing everything from medicine to animal fodder, and recruiting capable veterinarians to see to the health of over-worked animals.[54]

As Nogales helped improve the flow of essential supplies during the last half of 1915, the worst of the large-scale Armenian deportations and massacres were ending. Nogales, however, had a ringside seat for the inhumanities that remained. This was especially true after his responsibilities were increased to include assisting a Turkish colonel who was using Armenian and Greek labor battalions to rebuild a nearby military highway. This individual, Nogales recalled, stole enthusiastically from his own men and passing civilian refugees alike, neglecting nothing in the way of greed. Though Nogales claims to have improved conditions for laborers and punished venal military subordinates, he never directly challenged the crimes of his new superior and, after about four months, requested a leave that he later said was due to "nervous exhaustion." The leave was granted in November, and Nogales spent much of the remainder of 1915 in and around Jerusalem.[55]

During his travels, Nogales' fluent German helped his close association with German and Austrian officers in major cities like Damascus; just as his by-now fluent Turkish enabled him to hear information – good, bad, or indifferent – rarely provided to those perceived as foreign in any society. Much as Nogales understood his own cultural isolation and vulnerability, he did not broaden his understanding of this same situation to most Armenian males, whom he saw as petty, unscrupulous, and cowardly. Long before Psychology was an academic subject or before research about social and political isolation as conformity and social control mechanisms in Nazi concentration camps was ever undertaken, Nogales could not understand why Armenian males outside Eastern Anatolia did not

54 Nogales, 140-144
55 ibid.,151, 163.

rise up and rebel whenever possible during deportation proceedings. He was as un-empathetic to Armenian nationalism as he was to most individual Armenians. By "wasting time on ridiculous intrigues and a still more ridiculous period of waiting for the Entente [of Britain, France, Russia, and Italy] to act," instead of boldly attacking everywhere they could, Armenia had forfeited its chance at national independence or respect. "If, then, I use the word 'compassion,'" Nogales wrote, "it is not to the fate of the Armenian men that I feel like applying it, but to the women and innocent children who had to pay with their lives for the selfish cowardice of husband and father."[56]

Strong stuff, indeed. Also, however, a strong indicator that Nogales was hardly partial to narratives featuring Armenians as victims; and, so, when clear stories of murder and victimization occurred, they were hardly told out of any special sympathy for those victimized.[57]

Halil Again

Nogales' leave in the Holy Land was brief. Halil, his chief antagonist, soon reappeared to further complicate his military existence, and in an unlikely fashion. Late in 1915, Field Marshall von der Goltz was appointed commander in chief of the Turkish Sixth Army fighting in Mesopotamia. British forces had begun pushing Ottoman troops up

---

56 ibid.,148. Significant post-Holocaust studies of conformity to illegal rules began in the 1950's. For a discussion, see, i.e. Stanley Millgram, *Obedience to Authority: An Experimental View* (New York, Harper and Row, 1974). For very good studies of why other very-exploited groups very rarely rebelled, see, i.e., Dr. Elie A. Cohen, *Human Behavior in the Concentration Camp* (New York, W. W. Norton, 1953); Eugen Kogon, *The Theory and Practice of Hell: The German Concentration Camps and the System Behind Them* (New York, Farrar Straus, 1947) and Stanley Elkins, *Slavery: A Problem in American Institutional and Intellectual Life*, (Third edition, Chicago, University of Chicago Press, 1976).
57 For the standard Armenians as wholly victims narrative, see, i.e., Ben Kiernan, *Blood and Soil: A World History of Genocide and Extermination from Sparta to Darfur.* (New Haven, Yale, 2007).

the Tigris and Euphrates towards Baghdad. Until the end of October, the British offensive went well. Then, at Ctesiphon, just south of Baghdad, a new Turkish commander, Nur-ud-Din (Nurrutin), started pushing British forces back until, in December, about 11,000 British and Imperial troops were ordered to fortify a bend in the Euphrates at Kut-el-Amara to await relief. Nur-ud-Din promptly began a siege. Initial bloody attacks failed. Von der Goltz arrived; and, after consultations, a key decision was made to starve the British out at Kut while fortifying lines of entrenchments on both sides of the river below Kut to keep British reinforcements from reaching the besieged army under General Charles Townshend.[58]

At this point, several things happened. First, Halil arrived and replaced Nur-ud-Din. Then Halil theatrically and unfairly cast himself as victor over the English. To further increase his "borrowed" status and repute, Halil began isolating von der Goltz, titular head of the Sixth Army. Simultaneously, Nogales was ordered by Lieutenant-Colonel Kress von Kressenstein to go to assist von der Goltz in mid-December, 1915.[59]

Results were predictable, and Nogales' career in Mesopotamia was brief. It did not help that von der Goltz threatened to resign his command unless Armenian deportations were halted as Nogales was floating down the Tigris from Mosul to Baghdad on a wooden raft to join his staff. Once in Baghdad, however, Nogales took care to assist his chances of success as a staff officer by building personal relationships with people who could help him. Von der Goltz's top German aide Lieutenant Colonel von Restorff, for instance, had lived in Argentina. "Hardly a night passed," therefore, "without [he and Nogales] conversing for a while in Spanish." Charming officer gossips became serviceable military friends. An energetic young German aviator soon had Nogales on-hand helping him mend several

---

58 Millar, op cit.

59 Nogales, pp. 163-64. Edward J. Erikson, *Ottoman Army Effectiveness in World War I* (London, Routledge, 2007) pp. 94-96. Also gives Nur-ud-Din (Nurrutin) credit for the Ottoman victory at Kut-el-Amara.

captured English biplanes and then taking a trial flight in one of them that almost dumped both men in the Tigris when the plane's motor stalled. Thinking about the religious intolerance he had recently observed en route to Baghdad in Tikrit, he thought it proved that Christian converts to Islam were the most chauvinist, and further, that:

> Therein lies the reason why the most frightful massacres were perpetrated precisely in the cities of Sairt, Bitlis, Van, and Djarbekir [in Eastern Anatolia], whose population was largely composed of descendants of one-time Christian Armenians. The same thing occurred in the case of the *Laz* or tribesmen of the mountains of Trebizond on the Black Sea coast, who, not more than forty years ago, were converted from Christianity into the most intolerant Mohammedanism of the Ottoman Empire.[60]

Nogales, plainly, was no romantic ethno-historian who saw peoples or cultures as stable entities enduring without change and operating over millennia. Asia Minor, like his native Latin America, was a land of cultural overlays, transformations and mixtures: some of them explosive. It was also a land of what Northern Irish and Irish poet Seamus Heavey called "exact and tribal, intimate revenge."[61]

Revenge, moreover, was precisely what Nogales feared from Halil – for leaving his Anatolian command six months before. So, as in Aleppo, Nogales sought to interpose influential German officers between himself and Halil. This was the best – indeed only – protection he had. Among German staff officers in Baghdad, this was easy. They, however, did not command troops in battle at the front, where Nogales also, as earlier in Anatolia, wanted to be. So he got von der Goltz, in February, to commission him as an instructor and "personal representative" to a brigade of Turkish cavalry that

60 Nogales, pp. 183, 105, 180-81.
61 Seamus Heaney, "Punishment", in: *Selected Poems, 1965-1975* (London, Faber and Faber, 1980), p. 117.

Turkish non-commissioned cavalry officers.

operated directly under von der Goltz's orders. With this "extremely precious document," Nogales could fight the English without having to worry about political general Halil, who was outside his chain of command.[62]

This neat bureaucratic manipulation was very clever, but it did not last long. Halil and von der Goltz soon differed about tactics; Halil – who had little use for German officers – also made it known (in Turkish) that he thought little of von der Goltz. This was at a time when Turkish troops built layers of defensive works – to Goltz and Nur-ud-Din's plan – that exhausted a series of repeated British attacks. Nogales claims he protested this criticism of a superior to Halil's face, only to have a top-ranking Turkish officer and chief of staff in the Sixth Army promptly exercise revenge by ordering him into a Turkish cavalry unit not under Goltz's control. Ignoring Goltz's orders, the chief of staff allowed Turkish orders counted, not German. Nogales then lost his temper, and told the chief of staff just what he thought of Young Turk officers with more political ambition than military experience or brains. For the second time Nogales again sought his "discharge from the army for reasons of health."[63]

Helped by "strained relations" between German military representatives and Halil's officers, von der Goltz's aide von Restorff now came to Nogales' assistance. The aged Field Marshall then signed another "precious paper" releasing the Venezuelan from further Ottoman military service. The remainder of Nogales' narrative of this period in Mesopotamia has some overly dramatic features like a grateful von der Goltz personally awarding him an Iron Cross and a vengeful Halil trying to poison him. It also appears to make Nogales more important than he was. What is beyond debate is that Halil's political star was in the ascendancy within the Young Turk wartime regime. Von der Goltz was also dead of typhus on April 19, 1916. Less than two weeks after that, Kut surrendered to Halil: the inheritor of Nur-ud-Din and von der Goltz's earlier military decisions, tactics and strategies.[64]

As General Townshend surrendered his small army on April 29, however, a bit of quite real historical melodrama occurred about which there is now ample historical record. Two young British intelligence officers, a politically and socially prominent Colonel Aubrey Herbert, M.P. and a then – unknown Major T. E. Lawrence, arrived at Halil's headquarters on one of the more bizarre missions of the war. Their task was to bribe the victorious Turkish general to let all his captives go free. At this point, the British had no military advantages to trade. The Turks had fought them off on one front while starving them out on another. The Ottoman victory at Kut closely resembled what Julius Caesar's Roman legions had done to the Gauls at Alesia in 52 B.C. Offering a huge bribe to Halil as if he was a tribal Oriental potentate only accented British military failure. It also spoke volumes about British assumptions (which Nogales

---

63 ibid., p. 204.
64 ibid., 204-5, and 185ff (for strained relations).

shared) about widespread corruption within the topmost ranks of the Young Turk regime.[65]

Following Halil's quick dismissal of British bribery overtures totaling the then-impressive sum of £2 million, Lawrence secretly recorded his impressions of Nogales' "chief antagonist" Halil. Aged thirty-five, Halil appeared to Lawrence to be courageous, strong-willed, and fearless of consequences of his actions – not least because of his close family relationship with Enver. He was also alert, and a quick study. On the negative side, Halil was "restless and impatient," not exceptionally clever, "bored with details," and potentially rash. His Turkish chief of staff, Lawrence concluded, "probably supplied the brains and caution which are perhaps Halil's weak points."[66]

Unfortunately for Lawrence, British policy in Mesopotamia allowed no room for mobilizing Arab opposition to Turkish leaders like Halil. Halil thought so little of Arab soldiers in the Ottoman army, for example, that he refused even to discuss including them in Turkish prisoner exchanges agreed to for over a thousand severely wounded British and Indian troops at Kut. Arab disregard for Turkish leaders like Halil was thoroughly mutual. As Lawrence returned to Cairo, this failure to concern themselves with restive Arab portions of the Ottoman Empire was not a mistake he wanted to see British leaders repeat in Arabia or Syria.[67]

---

65 Millar, op cit., pp. 270ff; Turkish and German papers used the bribery effort to good account in subsequent weeks. Strict censorship kept any news from appearing in British papers. See: Jeremy Wilson, *Lawrence: The Authorized Biography of T. E. Lawrence* (New York, Atheneum,1990), pp. 272-73. and 254-78; *Caesar, The Gallic War* (Cambridge, Massachusetts, Loeb Classical Library, 1917 and reprinted), pp. 479 ff.

66 Philip Knightley and Colin Simpson, *The Secret Lives of Lawrence of Arabia* (New York, McGraw Hill, 1970), pp. 51-52; Nogales, p. 92.

67 For the opposition to mobilizing Arabs in Mesopotamia, see: Wilson, op. cit, pp. 265ff.

Two Captured British Aviators

Had Rafael De Nogales known of Lawrence's secret assessments of Halil, he would have agreed with them. As Lawrence headed towards Kut-el-Amara, however, Nogales headed away from it and northwards to Mosul and northern Syria. As he did, his life interwove decisively with a few of the British and Imperial prisoners recently taken by Ottoman forces.

Two of these prisoners—both officers—had been captured during a dangerous mission to cut Turkish telegraph lines west and north of Baghdad in November of 1915. The pilot, Captain Thomas W. White of the Royal Australian Flying Corps, and his observer, Lieutenant Francis Yeats-Brown of the Indian Army, landed their temperamental Maurice Farman "Rumpety" aircraft without stalling it, only to knock part of a wing off in an unscheduled meeting with a telegraph pole. While committing what destruction they could, Arab irregulars surrounded them and then a squad of Turkish troops under a courteous sergeant saved them from possible execution by taking them prisoner.[68]

For the next two months, White and Yeats-Brown were imprisoned in Baghdad. There, as they saw it, Turks disliked Arabs; Arab feelings were negative about Turks; Germans were infuriated by Turks; Turks were impatient of Germans; and all were sometimes very hard-put to feed, clothe, or care for English or Imperial prisoners in adequate ways. An Ottoman army where medical care was often minimal and food and pay was often late too-often could not care for its *own* soldiers well. Individual Turkish officers provided acts of kindness to prisoners. But British officers (who had monthly allowances paid via Swiss intermediaries) fared far better than enlisted men; and all of the many British and Imperial prisoners who were

---

68 T. W. White, *Guests of the Unspeakable: The Odyssey of an Australian Airman - Being a record of Captivity and Escape in Turkey* (Sydney, Angus and Robertson, – second Australian edition, 1938), pp. 30-41; Francis Yeats-Brown, *Caught by the Turks* (New York, Macmillan, 1920), pp. 1-15

taken in the Kut-el-Amara battles suffered from illnesses in relatively unsanitary conditions. A long 250 mile march from Baghdad to Mosul further weakened many enlisted men's physical conditions. Dysentery and typhus claimed numerous victims.[69]

When English, Australian and Indian army officers like White and Yeats-Brown protested shortages of everything from soap to shoes and the deaths of their men to the Turkish officer who Yeats-Brown called a "tiny Tamerlane with a limp and a scowl and bandy legs" who often ruthlessly oversaw prisoners' affairs in Mosul, a grudge-fight began that soon had lethal results. Commandant Abdul Ghani Bey's repute was attacked. He took an even-harder line on discipline and order which only further alienated English officers used to deference and Australians or British Indian Army officers un-used to courtesy towards "non-European" enemies many saw as semi-civilized. In March, White, Yeats-Brown, and about a dozen fellow officers were put in wagons for the 800 kilometer/500 mile trip to Aleppo. Hundreds of their men, Indian, Australian and British, were meanwhile marched separately, suffering about eighty percent mortality rates.[70]

Their Commanders' mortality rate might have been even higher, but for Rafael De Nogales, who was passing through Mosul just as the officers left for Aleppo. Hearing a military rumor that the officer prisoners would be massacred en route, Nogales and a mysterious Afghan prince traveling incognito caught up with the column and insured no such assassination would happen. This accomplishment was not easy. Especially as Nogales had resigned his Ottoman commission and now had no official rank whatsoever.

Nogales did not, however, lack for boldness. So, after introducing himself to surprised British officers in their own language and by presenting his card, inscribed "Rafael De Nogales – Caracas," he and his capable and well turned-out Turkish orderly, Tasim Chavush, or

69 White, op. cit., 72 ff; Yeats-Brown, op cit, 26ff.
70 Yeats-Brown, pp. 43-57; White, pp. 83-94.

Sergeant Tasim, took over command of the guard caravan. Playing what Australian Thomas White saw as a dangerous lone hand, Nogales ordered leaders along the way to provide food, shelter, and safety; while he and his mysterious Afghan companion shared whatever supplies they had or could purchase – many with military IOUs Nogales had no right to issue – with their prisoners. Passing ragged Turkish soldiers, many without boots, heading towards the front, the British officers kept their sick members well enough attended to, to continue traveling through miserable rainy weather. "He was unmindful of his own fate," Yeats-Brown later recalled about Nogales, "but took a sportsmanlike interest in ours. Some of his experiences had seared deep into his sensitive and romantic mind: a mind curiously at variance with his life."[71]

Australian aviator Thomas White, too, wondered at Nogales' mix of the chivalrous and the courageous with his loyalty to the "unspeakable" Turk. It was "incomprehensible" to White that the same man who saved him and his fellow officers in early 1916 should have so energetically killed Armenians at Van the year before. The only explanation White could provide in the first edition of his later war memoir was that "in a character so cosmopolitan and inured to cruelty the best attributes could not survive."[72]

---

71 Francis Yeats-Brown, *Bloody Years: A Decade of Plot and Counter-Plot by the Golden Horn* (New York, Viking, 1932), p. 151); White, op. cit., p. 98.
72 Thomas White, *Guests of the Unspeakable* (London, John Hamilton, 1928. This statement, significantly, was dropped in both subsequent Australian editions of White's book, in 1932 and 1935. For White's later and very prominent Australian political career which included being a Cabinet officer, candidate for prime minister, and Australian ambassador to London, see: Fred and Elizabeth Brenchley, *White's Flight: An Australian Pilot's Epic Escape from Turkish Prison-Camp to Russia's Revolution* (Milton, Queensland, John Wiley of Australia, 2004). For Yeats-Brown's prominent post-war literary and journalistic career which included one book very-loosely adapted into a Hollywood action film, see: John Evelyn Wrench, *Francis Yeats-Brown 1886-1944* (London, Eyre and Spottiswoode, 1948).

What White and Yeats-Brown both underestimated is that the war in the Ottoman Empire, like rebellion in Latin America, often mixed fear, religion, poverty and cruelty. Prisoners, for example, were rarely taken because they could rarely be fed or easily transported to secure prisons. With Ottoman troops often marching to war without shoes and in rags, and pestilence rampant, keeping Allied prisoners, displaced Armenians, or others fed was hardly easy. Turks deferred to rank—and money—and officers like White usually survived. Only two of the nine Australian aviation mechanics who kept White's planes flying were so lucky. They died of wounds, starvation, and disease, like seventy percent of all British prisoners, and one-third of Kut prisoners overall.[73]

Nogales parted from his prisoners shortly before they reached the rail line that would carry them to Aleppo. Later all the captured officers safely reached their final destination about 250 miles south of Constantinople after further assistance from a Turkish prison commandant in Aleppo, who had never even been told they were en route from Mosul. Nogales, meanwhile, had to save himself. All the military orders (and IOUs) he'd issued en route from Mosul were fraudulent. Suspicions grew. At Nisibin on today's Turkish-Syrian border, an Armenian telegrapher he'd earlier befriended told him that two English-speaking Ottoman physicians had been ordered to spy on what he was saying to the captives. Recalcitrant mayors he'd threatened with his pistol to provide food or lodging had complained.[74]

Nogales, ironically, was now safer back in the Ottoman army than he was outside it. So he was told by friendly Ottoman officers, Enver, besides, still did not want him to leave. He also still had the support

---

73 See, i.e., Millar, p. 284. Brenchley, pp. 109-10. Turkish soldiers, to provide perspective, had no dogtags. Nor did the Ottoman forces have a graves' registration bureau to bury the dead or to notify or to return mementoes to bereaved families. Hundreds of thousands of men simply disappeared into the maw of war and never returned to their villages.

74 White (1935), pp. 110 ff; Brenchley, p. 86; Nogales, 215-17.

and protection of the German military mission. His status as a Latin American volunteer to Turkey and Germany's cause still had propaganda value. So he decided to accept the inevitable and stay. Again, he was assigned to the Syria-Palestine-Arabia front; and, again, he was posted as a supply and transport officer.[75]

For the rest of the year, from March to December of 1916, Nogales' life was relatively uncomplicated. Cemal, the Young Turk leader whose military fiefdom was mostly Syria-Palestine-Arabia, is presented by Nogales as a "puffed-up nullity" mostly interested in extortion. Nogales, meanwhile, presents himself as a capable supply, training, and logistics officer for various commanders. Not until January of 1917, however, was he assigned another military posting: to help reorganize a Turkish infantry regiment in cooperation with its German commander.[76]

Timing, here, was important. The Ottoman army was starting to unravel from combat losses. In July and August of 1916, veteran Turkish regiments victorious at Gallipoli were "thrown away" in disastrous and ill-planned attacks against the Russians in Anatolia. This marked the final major Ottoman offensive of World War I. Halil, meanwhile, did not follow up the victory at Kut with attacks to dislodge British forces from southern Iraq or to cut the oil supplies essential to the British fleet flowing through oil pipelines in southern Iran to the shores of the Persian Gulf. Instead, Halil gave the British time to recover. They did exactly this. Then they took Baghdad on a second attempt in March, 1917: destroying most of Halil's army while so engaged. Simultaneously, large British forces built a railroad and a water pipeline across coastal Sinai and approached Turkish defenses on the Egyptian-Palestinian front around Gaza. Only the slow disintegration of the Russian army after revolution overthrew the Czar in March of 1917 and then the subsequent Bolshevik Revolution of October, 1917 took Russia completely out of the war

75 Nogales, 218-9.
76 ibid, 228-9.

Turkish infantry.

made Turkish military advance possible anywhere. Ottoman forces, Liman von Sanders later wrote, were fighting on too many fronts trying to accomplish too many things with far too few resources. Turkey, literally, was bleeding to death. A very good early overview of Turkey's participation in World War I concluded that: "...of the able-bodied men who saw active service at the front only from ten to twenty percent returned to their villages." With the unknown figures from the Gallipoli campaign excluded, about eight times as many Ottoman troops died from diseases like typhus, dysentery, and malaria as died from wounds.[77]

By early 1917, then, the Ottoman Empire needed every skilled military organizer it could get. So off to the battle fronts Nogales went, in part because another romantic military loner had arrived there a few months before him.

77 Erickson, op. cit., pp. 131-33, 176-77; von Sanders, op cit., pp. 326. Ahmed Emin Yalman, *Turkey in the World War* (New Haven, Yale University Press, 1930), pp. 252-53.

The Arab Revolt

Two men who understood early just how overextended the Ottoman Empire was were T. E. Lawrence and the Emir of Mecca, Hussein. Even before the war, Abdullah, one of Hussein's four sons, had sounded out the British about their support, in case his father used his powerful symbolic position as traditional governor of the holiest city in Islam to declare a jihad against the Turks. In April of 1914, British officials in Cairo were uninterested. Two years later, after major defeats at Turkish hands at Gallipoli and Kut, anything that could assist disloyalty within the one-third of the Ottoman army that was Arab had become a major concern. Late in June of 1916, the Emir began his revolt. Turkish forces were defeated in Mecca and at nearby Jiddah, Arabia's major port. Elsewhere, however, they hung on and began counterattacking, particularly along the 400 miles of the "Hijaz Railway" linking Medina with Damascus. In October, T. E. Lawrence went down the Red Sea to help arrange greater degrees of British military and financial support for Hussein's now-stalled "Arab Revolt".[78]

Lawrence's relative fluency in Arabic and sympathy for Bedouin folkways soon made him an important link in the money and materiel funneled to Hussein's uprising, as the British sought to expand nomadic raids into a Pan-Arab regional uprising. Leaving the essential military work of training Hussein's regular army and employing imported artillery, armored car, and airplane forces to others, Lawrence concentrated on organizing Arab raiding parties. Bedouin irregular cavalry cut Turkish communications and attacked small and scattered Turkish posts along over-extended Ottoman lines of communication and supply. Lawrence's major tasks involved selecting tribal leaders to conduct raids wisely and rewarding them promptly for jobs well done.[79]

---

78 Stewart, 140-141; Knightley and Simpson, 64ff; Wilson, 305ff; T. E. Lawrence, *Seven Pillars of Wisdom: A Triumph* (Garden City, New York, Doubleday Doran, 1935), pp. 72 ff.

Lawrence, who initially impressed his intelligence colleague Aubrey Herbert as "...an odd gnome, half cad with a touch of genius," was as prone as Nogales was to embroider his own self importance. He understood, however, that the Ottoman Empire, the only major Islamic power on Earth, did not want to give up its long-standing claim to being the guardian of the holiest sites in Islam; and that this, moreover, put them in the militarily dangerous position of having a long open flank along 300 miles of open desert ideal for guerilla operations on a military front where airplanes were very scarce. The observation was hardly unique with Lawrence. Nor did Lawrence, despite later claims, create an already obvious strategy.[80]

Instead, Lawrence recruited British experts in demolition and machine guns, started employing and supplying dependable Arabs, and used lightly armed raiding parties for the obvious purpose of blowing up Turkish railroads, bridges, and locomotives. Not until Lawrence and a group of Bedouin raiders – led by tribal chieftain Auda abu Tayi – seized the small Red Sea port of Aqaba on July 6, 1917 did Lawrence's military reputation really begin to shine. This was partly because Arab forces conquered two small Turkish garrisons without direct British aid; and partly because heroes of the traditional chivalric and knightly variety were very rare by this point in the war. The fact that Lawrence had knocked himself unconscious during the final cavalry charge of the Aqaba campaign after mistakenly shooting his own camel in the head was a detail rarely worthy of heroic wartime mention.[81]

---

79 Malcolm Brown, *Lawrence of Arabia: The Life the Legend* (London, Thames and Hudson, 2004), p. 40

80 Because of the political and religious nature of the Ottoman strategy in Arabia, 11,000 Turkish troops remained in Medina until after Turkey left the war. On January 10, 1919, they finally seized their general and surrendered. See, i.e., Mark Sykes to Aubrey. Herbert, circa October, 1914, in: Margaret FitzHerbert, *The Man Who Was Greenmantle: A Biography of Aubrey Herbert* (London, John Murray, 1983), pp. 147-48 and 144 (Lawrence characterization).

Again, timing was crucial. Lawrence the lowly liaison officer became Lawrence the leader of the Arab Revolt, in British eyes, because he claimed to have originated strategic and tactical ideas, because he had a very good sense of theatre and personality, and – especially – because heroes were in demand. Here was a Robin Hood of the desert, winning pre-industrial victories without hecatombs of dead. This, immediately after the bloody futilities of the battles of the Somme (1.5 million casualties from July to November of 1916) and Verdun (300,000 dead and 1 million wounded from February to December of 1916). Moreover, Lawrence's raids were fought on a Middle East front where cavalry charges in the grand manner unhindered by strafing airplanes or barbed wire entanglements still happened; where fronts were fluid and dynamic and where individual heroism and leadership had not been largely negated by machine guns, poison gas, tanks, and other tools of high technology war. Here too was a hero who could be – and was – advertised to Americans just reluctantly entering the war after April of 1917. Because, for instance, Lawrence was operating on a front where liberation of the holiest sites of Christianity from Muslim control for the first time since the end of the Crusades was – now – also advertised as a major war aim.[82]

The Battles of Gaza

The victory of the Arab irregulars in the Aqaba campaign of July 1917 against tiny garrisons numbering in the hundreds also contrasted with previous British experience against the main body of the Ottoman

81 Lawrence (1935), pp. 307-12; For a survey of Lawrence's embellishments that is not without sympathy and understanding, see: Suleiman Mousa, *T. E. Lawrence: An Arab View* (London and New York, Oxford University Press, 1966).

82 After Aqaba, for example, Lawrence dealt directly with the top British military commander in Egypt, and no longer through British-Intelligence or Arab leaders. He also got special funds he could use independently. U.S. publicist Lowell Thomas, as we shall see, was crucial to the mythmaking about "Lawrence of Arabia" that shortly ensued.

army numbering in the tens of thousands several hundred miles north. At the First and Second Battles of Gaza in March and April of 1917, efforts to break through undermanned Turkish divisions bolstered by Austro-Hungarian artillery and German machine gun detachments failed. Nogales almost missed both Gaza battles because the infantry unit he was training was scheduled to depart for Aqaba, until the decision was reversed. Then, in January, 1917, he finally got a long sought-after assignment to the staff of the Third Division of Ottoman Imperial Cavalry.[83]

Cavalry was traditionally an aristocratic military specialty; and so it was in the Ottoman army as well. Though generally partial to German over Turkish officers above the rank of major, Nogales was very enthusiastic about his new division commander, Lieutenant-Colonel Esat Bey, calling him "the personification of culture and chivalry." His fellow officers included the Ottoman Sultan's nephew (a squadron commander) and representatives of "distinguished families in Constantinople, men of intelligence and high traditions." Elite patrician military circumstances were a decided improvement over bloody and no-quarter street fighting in Van.[84]

Nogales nevertheless needed all the enthusiasm he could get now that he was back in his favorite branch of the service. Ottoman supply lines too-rarely supplied items like clothing and medicines. Arab troops sometimes had to have machine guns trained on them to prevent desertion. Outposts were crushed as the British used their complete naval superiority to build a railroad and a water pipeline towards Turkish lines along the northern coast of the Sinai Peninsula. Losses and disease had reduced the strength of nearby Turkish units to a third or less of their regulation numbers.[85]

Morale within Nogales' division, however, was high. Esat Bey, Nogales wrote, had rebuilt the division "with an abundance of energy

83 Nogales, op. cit., pp. 237-38, 242.
84 ibid., pp. 245, 249-50.
85 ibid, pp. 252-53.

Bedouin volunteers mounted on camels on the Sinai front.

and initiative amazing in an Oriental." Part of that command initiative involved Esat's giving Nogales the wide grant of authority he always craved in whatever military circumstances he operated. Von Kress of the Fourth Army general staff only added to Nogales' satisfaction when he asked him to lead a small Turkish raiding party through 150 kilometers of enemy territory to dynamite a major British water pumping station. Failing in the effort because of unusually large concentrations of British troops advancing to the front, Nogales arrived back at his base in Beersheba on March 25, to discover the First Battle of Gaza beginning. Taking charge of a column of ammunition, supplies, and reinforcements, Nogales brought them to the left side of the Turkish line; where his unit was deployed to stop efforts to swing inland around Gaza, a highly fortified town astride the major land route between Syria and Egypt. As "British airplanes cut the air like steely dragonflies" bombing horses and men, Nogales participated in the early stages of an advance against British and Australian cavalry, aimed at discomfiting British movement along an "extensive front, some thirty kilometers wide, enveloped in thick smoke from which burst incessant tongues of flame and through which tore the smoking arcs of the shells." Here, finally, was the sort of grand battle experience Nogales had gone to Europe over a year and a half before to find.[86]

Grandeur, however, came at a heavy price: 4,000 British casualties and 1,500 Turkish (including deserters). Arab levies, which Nogales generally thought useless in war, waited until night fell to slay wounded enemy soldiers on the battlefield and steal money and clothing from the dead. Supply problems continued. Little grain reached the horses and limited Turkish scouting and raiding operations. Overall, Nogales wrote, Ottoman cavalry had been "reduced to almost nothing, through official peculation and the starvation and general neglect of the mounts." Hunger, disease, and corruption had combined to make Nogales' relatively-affluent unit an exception, not a rule. British superiority in all major men and material areas was steadily growing.[87]

Climax

On April 18, British forces approached Turkish outposts again in strength; and, the next day, the Second Battle of Gaza commenced. This time, British infantry and artillery attacked mainly in the center of the Turkish lines inland from Gaza and the coast. Battle particularly roiled around a redoubt approximately three kilometers / two miles from Nogales' unit, which, again, was on the Turkish forces' left wing. As counterattacks drove the British center back, and conflict intensified, the Third Cavalry Division was ordered to make a subsidiary push straight against British cavalry and mounted infantry on the right of the British lines. Because of outlying British cavalry on low hills to their left, Nogales believed the order to advance against enemies to their front was suicidal, in that their flank was exposed and the possibility of being taken in the rear as they advanced was very immediate. The looks of "unmoved control" and "utter

86 ibid., 259-272
87 ibid., 275-276.

fearlessness" on the faces of his fellow Turkish officers, however, became "one of the most cherished memories" of Nogales' Ottoman military service.[88]

The Third Cavalry then attacked with sufficient dash to drive Australian and New Zealand mounted troops back until enemy machine guns and light artillery stopped further Turkish advance. At this point, Nogales took a squadron of troops and eighty Bedouin and swung around to the south to flank the screen of machine gun detachments behind which Australian cavalry was regrouping. This caused the 5th and the 7th Australian Light Horse and the 2nd British Light Horse to retreat further before finally bringing the Turkish forces to a halt, again with machine guns. Shortly afterwards, and after taking a total of 6,000 casualties in "the most considerable battle" yet fought on the Egypt-Arabia front, the British commander retreated, in the face of a Turkish force half his size.[89]

Nogales later enthused that his Division's attack had turned the tide of battle. The official British war history differed; it gave primary credit to a stubborn defense by Turkish infantry and their willingness to counterattack, while also recognizing the cavalry – and Nogales. Australia's official military history was far less complimentary. In it, Australian cavalry had not really been forced to retreat at all. Instead a large Turkish force had cravenly lurked out of range of a much smaller Australian one, and only advanced "behind a screen of Arab rabble." Turkish cavalry, moreover, were "indifferently led, mounted on a nondescript lot of ponies which were usually in wretched condition," and "too timid to be effective" at anything, even scouting. The modern Turkish official history of the Palestine campaign does not mention Nogales at all.[90]

---

88 Sir George MacMunn and Cyril Falls, *History of the Great War Based on Official Documents: Military Operations Egypt and Palestine: From the Outbreak of War with Germany to June, 1917* (London, His Majesty's Stationery Office, 1928), pp 326 ff; Nogales, op. cit., 281.
89 MacMunn and Falls, *Military Operations...*, pp. 343 if, esp. 345-46; Nogales, op. cit., pp. 282-83.

Second Battle of Gaza
Vanguard of Turkish 3rd Imperial Cavalry Division.

Culmination and Withdrawal

Fortunately, Nogales was not dependent upon the apparently selective memories of Australian cavalry officers for his sense of military self-worth. Finally, he had the experience of military victory and chivalry in the grand style that he had long craved, in a major battle against cavalry units of the world's most-powerful empire. No longer was the politically exiled Venezuelan a supply officer, an escort of Arab deserters, a fighter of Armenians, a trainer of infantry, or caught up in the "vicious circle called Staff – which has no beginning and no end, and in which one can never attain perfection." Amidst shot and shell, Nogales had finally proven himself to himself.[91]

90 H. S. Gullett, *The Australian, Imperial Force in Syria and Palestine, 1914-1918* (1923) (University of Queensland Press and Australian War Memorial reprint edition, 1983), pp. 332-33. Nogales, op. cit., p. 289. Ed Erickson kindly told me about Nogales' non-existence in the Turkish official military history of the Palestine campaign.
91 Nogales, op. cit., pp. 285, 268, 245, 242.

After the Second Battle of Gaza, the British commanding general in the Egypt-Arabian theater was replaced. British cavalry and aviation attacks meanwhile kept the pressure on Turkish positions. Transportation and other infrastructure were improved. The British did not lack for railroads, tanks, barbed wire, food, medicine, and water pipelines – while the Ottoman forces did. New British commander-in-chief General Edmund Allenby reorganized troops and increased the scope of Arab raids via £200,000 per month payments to Lawrence. The British would very definitely be back.[92]

The hot summer weather between May and September, however, inhibited large scale military activities. In that relatively peaceful interim, Nogales was ordered to organize a small independent cavalry expedition to scout and raid British forward positions in the Sinai desert. From May 10 until early June, he and an almost completely Arab force of regulars and irregulars, traveling by night, undertook guerilla war and sought to reaffirm Ottoman sovereignty over interior desert tribes. His major effort was against desert oases and wells and the British coastal military railroad in the neighborhood of El Arrish, about 100 miles west of Gaza. If Nogales' 150-200 men – many from El Arrish – could disrupt these, he hoped to draw away enemy cavalry from further attacks that Allenby was planning against Turkish fortifications stretching between Gaza and Beersheba. Colonel White, while in a prisoner of war camp in Turkey, heard that Nogales had led daring raids on British communications from another captured member of the Australian Flying Corps who had spoken with Nogales and others in Palestine.[93]

Initially, Nogales and his men avoided detection, while firming-up alliances with local Bedouin tribes and threatening or killing those leaders supporting the British. Once his camp was located by British

---

92 For Allenby, see: Lawrence James, *Imperial Warrior: The Life and Times of Field Marshal Viscount Allenby 1861-1936* (London, Weidenfield and Nicolson, 1993); Archibald Percival Wavell, *Allenby: A Study in Greatness* (New York Oxford University Press, 1941).
93 Nogales, op. cit., pp. 291-305; White (1928), pp. 118-19.

scout-planes, however, his raiders also went out on night dynamiting missions against British installations. This stirred-up an intense British response. A German staff officer later told him that "the main body of the enemy cavalry" had gone off in pursuit of his raiding party. Claiming too much for the importance of his mission, Nogales nevertheless got his men back alive out of a risky situation, and made the attack Allenby later successfully made against the southernmost portion of the Turkish line at Beersheba more difficult. None of what Nogales' raid accomplished, however, changed the problems of corrupt and insufficient supply lines, a lack of elementary defensive technology (including barbed wire), and a growing imbalance of military power. As he headed back to Turkish lines, he realized that "the Turkish banner was leaving Egyptian soil forever."[94]

Nogales, too, soon left the battle front. First, an ear infection caused him to go to Jerusalem for treatment. Once in the rear, he saw the effects of growing corruption and "the ruin caused by deportations, epidemics, and looting." With the United States now in the war, Nogales – who had lived in the U.S.A. for at least 10 years – knew that economic and military imbalances would only grow. Though the U.S.A. never declared war against the Ottoman Empire, additional pressure on Germany on the Western Front in Europe insured that if supplies of essentials like locomotives, rails, and communications dried-up, it would further worsen Turkish supply and reinforcement problems. The British were meanwhile conquering Baghdad, and Enver was invading the Caucasus with troops desperately needed elsewhere seeking the will-of-the-wisp of Turkish unity, against the advice of better and more realistic military men like Mustafa Kemal. It was time for Nogales the realist to leave. Via a Turkish lieutenant-colonel with good political connections, Nogales got an order from the Turkish high command in Damascus giving him permission to leave for military reassignment in Constantinople.[95]

---

94 ibid., p. 309.

The End of the Ottomans

For all practical purposes, Nogales was now out of the war. From June, 1917 until Turkey signed an armistice on October 30, 1918, Nogales was either inspecting cavalry units being formed in Anatolia, training cavalry guarding the Sultan, studying everything from heavy artillery to aviation reconnaissance in Constantinople, or visiting wartime acquaintances in Germany and the Austro-Hungarian empire. His growing appreciation of important military innovations of World War I like aviation clarified that the good old days of cavalry charges – or mounted raids into Venezuela from the Colombian border – were a thing of the past.[96]

Public support for the Young Turks, meanwhile, fell steadily. As many as 300,000 military deserters unsettled life in the Ottoman Empire. Allenby's defeat of Turkish forces at the Third Battle of Gaza in the week between October 31 and November 7th, 1917 was followed by the British occupation of Jerusalem on December 9. When the final offensive against remaining Turkish forces in Palestine and Syria came in September of 1918, some Ottoman units, previously among the best infantry of the war, had clearly lost the will to fight. Reasons were not far to seek. Food was so short that only front line troops, for example, were given "anywhere near enough to eat," admitted German General Liman Von Sanders. "We are like a cotton thread drawn across the enemy's path," Brigadier General Mustafa Kemal wrote – sadly but presciently – to his doctor in Constantinople just before Allenby's crushing attack. Within weeks, he and what remained of his men had retreated 100 miles and were fighting for their lives.[97]

When the cotton thread of what remained of the Ottoman Empire's armies parted in September and October of 1918, Nogales

---

95 ibid., p. 312.
96 ibid., p. 326.
97 Andrew Mango, *Ataturk: The Biography of the Founder Modern Turkey* (Woodstock, New York, Overlook Press, 2000) pp. 179-80, von Sanders, op. cit., pp. 265-66, 259.

was in Germany. Military friends advised against him returning to Constantinople, but he went anyway, claiming chivalric duty. Arriving the day after the Armistice was signed in a militarily-occupied city. Nogales had redeemed his word of honor as a neutral Venezuelan serving as an Ottoman officer. But he was now also largely without friends or protectors in a defeated and militarily occupied capital of a country soon to experience a huge Greek invasion.[98]

Several of the captured British officers Nogales had befriended on the road from Mosul to Aleppo early in 1916, however, now re-entered his life and came to his aid. On November 9, 1918, Captain E. J. (James) Fulton, a British aviator, invited Nogales to a dinner in Constantinople. He and fellow Captains Yeats-Brown and B. S. Atkins, Major H. C. Reilly of the Indian Army, and Lieutenant Commander Goad, said Fulton, perhaps should not have survived that journey without Nogales' "great kindness." So it seemed only proper to offer him a "bad dinner" in return.[99]

Letter to Nogales from E. J. (James) Fulton

The officers ended up giving Nogales far more than a dinner. They also got the British Military High Commission in Constantinople to

98 Nogales, op. cit. pp. 327-29.

provide Nogales passage to South America in April, 1919, instead of stranding him as an enemy alien in a country where the British were arresting Ottoman military men for "crimes against humanity" during the Armenian massacres and holding them – with others who had mistreated military prisoners of war – for trial. As he saluted his many fallen Ottoman, German, and Austrian comrades from the deck of the departing steamship, modern Turkish secular nationalism's greatest leader, Mustafa Kemal, was about to begin his successful war in Anatolia to save what remained of the empire as a national homeland for the Turks.[100]

Lines Drawn on Maps

As war loomed in Turkey, and an obscure Venezuelan officer left for the Americas, the remnants of the old Ottoman Empire were full of conflicting tribalisms, nationalisms, and imperialisms. The basic problem was that Britain had promised very much to very many to obtain and maintain anti-Ottoman alliances, and the promises conflicted. French claims overlapped Arab; Arab claims conflicted with Zionist; and so on. Meanwhile, the politics of international petroleum dominated everything else. All Arab sovereignty claims except in the sacred soil of the area around Mecca and Medina were secondary – because British control of the Middle Eastern oil that World War had shown to be essential for modern warfare and industry was primary. To get the French (and, later, the Americans) to accept minority holdings in new Iraqi fields around Kirkuk, for example, Feisal's kingdom in Syria was given to the French. What

99 A photograph of James' letter faces page 48 in the British edition of Nogales' *Memoirs of a Soldier of Fortune* (London, Wright and Brown, 1931 The data on the officers comes from Fred and Elizabeth Brenchley, op. cit., i.e., pp. 69, 62.
100 Akcam, op. cit. pp. 236-38. (UK military courts were created in late January, 1919.); Kaldone G. Nweihed, *The World of Venezuelan Nogales Bey/ Venezuelali Nogales Bey'in Dunyasi* (Ankara, Embassy of the Bolivarian Republic of Venezuela in Turkey, 2005), p. 122; Mango, op. cit., pp. 217 ff; Nogales, op. cit., 330.

Lawrence had early on termed a "political mosaic, a tissue of small jealous principalities incapable of cohesion and yet always ready to combine against an outside force" resulted from the Arab Revolt, almost all overseen and guaranteed by British power.[101]

This early and accurate power politics summary, however, was penned before Lawrence had ever fought and bled with Bedouin raiders. Political intelligence and combat officer T. E. Lawrence's subsequent loyalties were torn. Lawrence had lied to Arab leaders like Hussein on behalf of a British Empire in which he believed. "Better we win and break our word than lose," he later wrote in a carefully suppressed first chapter to his memoirs not published until 1939. But as the balance of military advantage shifted decisively against the Turks in late 1917 and early 1918, Lawrence had hoped to redeem his promises (and himself) by edging around the 1916 Sykes-Picot Agreement dividing conquered Ottoman Arab lands into a British and a French sphere of imperial control. Lawrence's efforts were various. He sought, for example, to recruit Zionist financiers to underwrite friendly Arab rulers to avoid strife over overlapping and conflicting promises in Palestine; or he proposed self-governing dominion status for Arab lands within the Empire. (Syria was to resemble Canada, not India.). To augment pro-Arab sovereignty arguments at the Versailles Peace Conference and within the British government, Lawrence also used external press and media pressure.[102]

---

101 Saudi Arabia was not an important source for oil until U.S. firms drilled the first successful wells in the late 1930s. Knightley and Simpson, op.cit., pp. 52-53; For petroleum and the war, see, i.e. Ludwell Denny, *We Fight for Oil* (New York and London, Alfred A. Knopf, 1928); Daniel Yergin, *The Prize: The Epic Quest for Oil, Money, and Power* (New York, Simon and Schuster, 1991, pp. 167ff.
102 Knightley & Simpson, op. cit., p. 159.

Heroism as Antidote to Moral Ambiguity

A key ally in this effort was American movie maker and publicist Lowell Thomas, who arrived in Europe in August of 1917 with the express purpose of increasing support for the new U.S. war effort. Enjoying government support both in Washington and London, Thomas intended to film an appealing young soldier in action and thus underline the war's heroic virtues. The mud and slaughter of the Western Front frustrated Thomas' initial efforts. His initial hero candidate was killed in action before he could even contact him. But Allenby's victory at the Third Battle of Gaza and his subsequent occupation of Jerusalem was an "event of the greatest importance" to help arouse the very Christian and religious United States "to complete support of the Allies." British officials knew a sympathetic propagandist when they saw one, and squired Thomas and his cameraman around. In Jerusalem in January of 1918, the same man who had earlier first accompanied Lawrence to Arabia introduced Thomas to Lawrence. Both immediately recognized the publicity advantages of the other. Thomas had his romantic Imperial hero leading unspoiled primitives to overthrow their oppressors; Lawrence had a cutting-edge visual means to reach potentially huge audiences on behalf of Arab leaders and himself.[103]

In March, 1918, Thomas spent two weeks in and around Aqaba with Lawrence, who insured he met Feisal and other Arab Revolt leaders. Films of camel charges were staged, as no fighting was underway. British War Office censorship was light, and Thomas moved on to spend the final months of the war on other fronts.[104]

---

103 Joel C., Hodson, *Lawrence of Arabia and American Culture: The Making of a Trans Atlantic Legend* (Westport, Conn., Greenwood Press, 1995, pp. 13-16; Wilson, op. cit., pp. 489-90; Knightley and Simpson, op. cit., pp. 1-2.
104 Hodson, op. cit., pp. 17-21); Wilson, op. cit., pp. 492-93.

Returning to the United States in February, 1919, Thomas immediately set to work on a notably successful media celebration entitled "With Allenby in Palestine and Lawrence in Arabia" that began showing in New York in March, 1919, shortly after the Versailles Peace Conference began. Propaganda still had important benefits in underwriting Anglo-American unity as very divisive post-war diplomatic issues were being decided. By

Lawrence in Bedouin kit

August, Thomas' dramatic narration of his silent movie documentary was playing in London, where it was a smash hit for five months. Lawrence became the shining hero who was the antidote to the suffering and moral ambiguity of the war. Daniel Boone and Davy Crockett came to the Middle East, in Thomas's wildly romanticized narrative, via Covent Garden and the Royal Albert Hall. The script came complete with imaginary adventures like Lawrence killing six Turks with a Colt revolver. More than a million people saw the show in London. Editors of newspapers like the *Times of London* and the *Manchester Guardian* suspended disbelief and lauded the show. Leading politicians like Winston Churchill, meanwhile, understood the (often religiously-imbued) political support "stars" like Lawrence provided to British power and imperial prestige.[105]

Lawrence, moreover, was a silent and willing accomplice in this wildly romanticized treatment of himself and the Arab Revolt. Privately, Lawrence occasionally complained about Thomas' "red-hot lying." Publicly, he said nothing. Personal reticence mixed with political calculation. Anything that underscored the Arab contribution to British victory might only aid their status in political bargaining. Over the next three years, Thomas' documentary played to four million people worldwide. Then Thomas spun a best-selling book, *With Lawrence in Arabia*, off his lecture series. Romantic imperial heroism, by now, was almost total. Thomas, for instance, wrote an imaginary chapter in which he had a group of untrained Bedouin women and children suddenly transformed into military paragons by Lawrence, to the point that they fought off a combined attack by Turkish regulars and machine gunners and German artillerymen and aviators at the ancient archaeological site of Petra in modern Jordan. Two hundred thousand people purchased this orientalist fantasy in Britain and the United States in the 20 years after its appearance, and it was still unchanged and in print in the U.S.A. as a non-fiction work as late as 1960.[106]

Lowell Thomas' tall tales didn't help fledgling Arab nationalism very much; but they made Thomas rich and Lawrence into the best-known British officer of World War I. Having used bad propagandistic means to accomplish what he believed were good (or good-enough) political ends, however, Lawrence was soon on the horns of howling personal dilemmas. Fame was a jealous mistress. Reporters pried for their livings, and Lawrence the illegitimate son had this and other things about himself to hide.

Hide them he did, first by withdrawing to a well-appointed and paid position at Oxford to write his memoirs, *Seven Pillars of Wisdom*.

105 Hodson, op. cit., p. 35; Wilson, op. cit., pp. 624-25.
106 Lowell Thomas, *With Lawrence in Arabia* (New York, Collier, 1924), Chapter 19, has the battle. See the paperback Popular Library editions of 1960 published in New York City, pp. 142-45, for the unaltered and utterly fantastic details; Wilson, op. cit., 625-6.

Finished in 1920, this "confessional work" overplayed Lawrence's military importance and featured, among other episodes, a homosexual rape involving a Turkish commander and prison guards at a Syrian outpost that seems to have owed as much to invention as reality. Printed in several infinitesimal and expensive editions affordable only by 100 wealthy and well-connected subscribers who paid at least one thousand of today's dollars apiece, Lawrence's mix of self-analysis and socio-political commentary remained a very private creation for a very restricted and elite readership until what Lawrence termed the "Boy Scout version" of *Seven Pillars* appeared as *Revolt in the Desert* in 1927.[107]

Lawrence, meanwhile, avoided the quandaries of fame by reinventing himself. After briefly advising Colonial Secretary Winston Churchill on postwar Arab policy in 1921 and 1922, Lawrence resigned, changed his name twice, and did his best to disappear from public notice entirely. Like Nogales, Lawrence saw aviation as the wave of the military future. So he enlisted in the Royal Air Force (RAF) initially as a candidate reconnaissance photographer. After "backing into limelight" with Lowell Thomas, Lawrence spent five years backing away from it with a vengeance in three military postings, until he was assigned as a clerk to an aircraft supply and repair depot in Karachi in modern Pakistan in 1927.[108]

---

107 Hodson, op. cit., p. 85; Jeffrey Meyers, "T. E. Lawrence in His Letters," in Meyers (ed.) *T. E. Lawrence: Soldier, Writer, Legend* (New York, St. Martin's, 1989), pp. 9ff.
108 T. E. Lawrence's *The Mint: Notes Made in the R.A.F. Depot* (New York, Doubleday, 1955) was the first appearance of Lawrence's story of these years.

Chapter Five

Nogales in Fame and Obscurity

As imperial hero Lawrence fled a secular hagiography he'd helped create, Rafael De Nogales had little fame to flee. Throughout the Americas, Turkey was, at best, a military, political, economic, and diplomatic afterthought. The Gomez dictatorship in neutral Venezuela did all it could to constrict the military or other celebrity of its exiled opponents. The United States, for its part, had never gone to war with the Ottoman Empire. Political pacification of the Middle East remained a British or French responsibility. American concerns in the region primarily involved Protestant missionaries and the protection of Christian holy sites and religious congregations. What little most Americans had ever heard about Turkey, accordingly, they did not especially like. Orphaned Armenians as a result of wartime massacres or starvation and expelled Greeks and Armenians following a failed Greek invasion of Asia Minor in 1920-1922 combined to create an image of an unstable and occasionally barbaric land. Few Turks immigrated to the U.S.A. between 1890 and 1924, and very few of those stayed. Most Americans had never met a Muslim, or a Turk. It was easy, accordingly, to believe almost anything about either.[109]

109 For immigration, see: John J. Grabowski "Prospects and Challenges: The Study of Early Turkish Immigration to the United States," *Journal of American Ethnic History* (Fall, 2005) pp. 85-100. (25,000 immigrated between 1890 and 1924; 20 percent of those stayed.) For foreign-born data, *Historical Statistics of the United States: Colonial Times to 1970* (Washington, DC, Government Printing Office, 1976), p. 117. For the importance of Armenian issues re: the restoration of full diplomatic relations between the U.S.A. and Turkey after the war, see: Robert L. Daniel, "The Armenian Question and American-Turkish Relations, 1914-1927." *Mississippi Valley Historical Review*, Vol. 46 (1959-1960), pp. 252-75.

These American perceptions were important because Rafael De Nogales spent large portions of his remaining life in the U.S.A. and wrote increasingly in English. The story all began with a book, a poetic editor and translator, and a revolutionary plot.

The book itself Nogales produced at a hacienda in Colombia, after failing to get permission to enter the United States between 1920 and 1922. Then the adventure began. Fearful that Nogales was writing a book against him and his regime, Dictator Juan Vicente Gomez initially tried to block his departure from Colombia. Nogales publicly protested, and later a Venezuelan consul issued him a new passport. Mocking Nogales as a crazy joke, Venezuelan consular officials on his path through Central America nevertheless kept close track of him. On August 2, 1922, his arrival in Panama with his war memoirs was noted. On the 14th, the consul reported that he had appealed to the German colony in Panama for lodging and transportation expenses on to Costa Rica. By February 10, 1923, he reached New York City and, on February 25, of that same year, he was first extensively profiled in *The New York Times* by fellow Venezuelan émigré and Harvard graduate T. R. Ybarra. His two-thirds of a page "Nogales Bey of Venezuela" story of about 1,500 words summarized Nogales' war experiences, exaggerations and all, and clearly demonstrated Nogales had honed his "daredevil" story-telling skills.[110]

Nogales' manuscript was in Spanish, however, and intended for a Venezuelan and Latin American audience. So on Nogales travelled to Germany, where he stayed with a German nobleman one of his sisters had married. There, he contracted with a Berlin, Madrid, and Buenos Aires-based publishing house that produced books for the Latin American market. In 1924, Editora Internacional published Nogales' *Four Years* in its original Spanish edition. The next year, another

110 De Trinca, op. cit., p. 70; T. R. Ybarra, "Nogales Bey of Venezuela," *New York Times*, February 25, 1923, p. SM - 10, 13. For Ybarra, see his memoirs, *Young Man of the World* (New York, Ives Washburn, 1942) and *Young Man of Caracas* (New York, Ives Washburn, 1941).

Berlin-based firm published a slightly shortened authorized German version of Nogales' war memoirs, minus graphic material about Armenian massacres including several photos of starved children and an unidentified execution placed in the Spanish version.[111]

Nogales' literary activities were watched. Venezuelan embassy officials asked German Foreign Ministry staff to suppress any book or pamphlet by Nogales critical of Gomez's regime. Venezuelan officials even got Nogales' Spanish language publisher to send them page proofs to insure no negative "veiled references" existed. When Nogales tried to slip in a prologue attacking the

General Juan Vicente Gomez, 1925

Gomez dictatorship in the final production stages of his book, the director of the press suppressed it, substituting a summary of Nogales' war service from a Berlin newspaper of September 15, 1918 instead. "There is no doubt," the ambassador reported back to Gomez and his secret police heads in Caracas on August 5, 1924,

> ... that Nogales is unbalanced but his adventurous character gives him a certain prestige among the people who only judge

111 Rafael De Nogales, *Cuatro Anos Bajo La Media Luna: Su Diario e Impressiones Durante La Guerra Mundial en Los Diversos Frentes de Europa y Asia* (Madrid, Berlin, Buenos Aires, Editora-Internacional, 1924) and *Vier Jahre unter dem Halbmond: Erinnerungen aus dem Weltkriege* (Berlin, Verlag von Reimar Hobbing, 1925. (The first volume has 31 chapters, the second 25).

by appearances, and as his book is exotic it will have a large circulation in Latin America, so the publication of the prologue that was suppressed would have had an undesirable effect.[112]

To further assure the suspicious (and almost illiterate) dictator of his devotion, the ambassador also insured that he received one of the first Spanish language copies of Nogales' war memoir, including the suppressed anti-Gomez prologue. He then denied Nogales a Venezuelan passport in September, Venezuela's legation in Italy then kept watch on Nogales' "ill-humored" movements and possible involvements in attempts to ship arms to Venezuela. Nogales' road to print, his Venezuelan biographer Mirela Quero de Trinca rightly remarks, was long and uneven. The German language edition of the book, like the Spanish version, said nothing at all about Nogales' homeland or its long-resident dictator.[113]

Gomez's large spy apparatus also insured that Nogales' first book was very rarely available in his homeland. In the United States, however, Nogales' literary standing was starting to flower. An important indication of this was the first of two positive reviews his first book received in *The New York Times*. On May 17, 1925, a long, sympathetic survey of Nogales' good humored "knight errantry" appeared, under the title "Rafael De Nogales, Soldier of Fortune." Written by bilingual poetess Muna Lee, the review was of the Spanish language edition of a book not then available either in English or in North America. How did it happen that one of the better respected newspapers on Earth reviewed a book about a little-known war written in a language very few *New York Times* editors or readers even understood?[114]

---

112 De Trinca, op. cit., p. 71, with thanks to James Pavlish for this translation. Many of De Trinca's primary sources are available in *Boletin Del Archivo Historico de Miraflores*, Numero 74, (Imprenta Nacional, Caracas, 1972), pp. 317-344.
113 ibid., p. 72.

Chronicles of Love and Revolution

The explanation owed much to Nogales' reviewer and her husband, and comparatively little to Nogales himself. In 1919, a romantic, talented, and widely published young poetess working in New York met and married a younger and even more ardent Puerto Rican poet and journalist named Luis Munoz Marin, son of the best-known Puerto Rican politician of the pre-World War I period. Raised largely in the United States and a graduate of Georgetown University, Munoz, at this point in his career, was a Socialist. He was also smitten by a multi-lingual pan American feminist as left-wing as he. Widely known, successful, and eminently sociable, the couple regularly opened their home to Sunday night parties. Their guests, poet and literary critic Horace Gregory later recalled,

> …were an extraordinary combination of Arctic explorers, European journalists, young New York writers, Spanish American military men, and soldiers of fortune; talk was of revolution, the wisdom of the Eskimos, reindeer meat, the novels of D. H. Lawrence and James Joyce, the poetry of Robinson Jeffers.[115]

Munoz and Lee's salon mixed the Pan-American, the poetic, the revolutionary, and the adventurous. In time it attracted Nogales, probably late in 1924 or early in 1925. "Dramatic raconteur" Nogales "held the gatherings spellbound with tales of his adventures." Enough so that even Earl Parker Hanson, a skeptical longtime political friend and ally of Munoz, failed to notice when Nogales embroidered reality (i.e., by claiming to have been a general in the Ottoman army).[116]

114 Muna Lee, "Rafael De Nogales, Soldier of Fortune: Descended From a Family of Conquerors, He Has Kept That Tradition Alive," *New York Times Book Review*, May-17, 1925, p. 7.
115 Gregory, as quoted in: Jonathan M. Cohen, *A Pan-American Life: Selected Poetry and Prose of Muna Lee* (Madison, University of Wisconsin Press, 2004), p. 24.
116 Earl Parker Hanson, *Transformation: the Story of Modern Puerto Rico* (New York, Simon and Schuster, 1955), p. 103.

Embroidery aside, Nogales nevertheless had military experience then very rare among Latin Americans. He had fought with and against the best European armies of his day. Muna Lee seems to have been genuinely taken with Nogales' courtesy, quiet-voiced drawing room manners, and ability to laugh at himself, all the while wrapping himself up in Spanish and Spanish-American warrior-intellectual traditions. So, as she reviewed Nogales' book in Spanish for *The New York Times*, she was also translating it into English, and using her many literary and editorial connections to help Nogales find a major New York publisher. One of Muna Lee's best friends, writer Constance Murray Skinner, also soon became Nogales' literary-agent.[117]

Muna Lee

---

117 ibid., p. 104; Rafael De Nogales to Constance Murray Skinner, May 20 1926. Constance Murray Skinner Papers, General Correspondence, Box 7, New York Public Library Literature Archives.

Constance L. Skinner

As his wife sacrificed her own poetic career to start, in her recent biographer's words, "giving a strong voice to others," Munoz Marin had his own un-poetic reasons for valuing the part-Indian *"Andino" (Andean)* Venezuelan. Nogales' military experience was precisely what he was looking for in his efforts to build Pan-American unity and the Pan-American organized labor movement. In 1920, Munoz had started cooperating with Santiago Iglesias, the leader of the Socialist Party in Puerto Rico. He and Iglesias had decided that Juan Vicente Gomez, the bloody-handed tyrant of Venezuela, was also "one of the great obstacles to the spread and success of that [labor-based socialist] movement, not only in Venezuela, but also, because of what he represented, in many other parts of Latin America."[118]

The Mexican Connection

The problem with Gomez was that he was another Porfirio Diaz, the self-made Caudillo who had ruled Mexico with an iron hand for 35 years until his overthrow in the first year of the Mexican Revolution of 1910-1920. Diaz had opened Mexico's doors wide to foreign businessmen, and insured no inconveniences like labor unions

---

118   Cohen, op. cit, p. 25; Hanson, op. cit, p. 102.

marred their operations. Huge tracts of country were legally or illegally granted to U.S. and British oil companies anxious to find new reserves. Diaz and his allies took their cut of the proceeds and kept the peace. Autocracy and economic growth went well together, in a sometimes ruthless fashion not at all unusual in today's era of multinational globalism.[119]

Once Diaz fell, however, an oil boom, revolutionary movements, and pandemic banditry all occurred simultaneously. Legalities were rarely on anybody's mind for long. Growing stability after 1917, however, opened the doors to Mexican trade unionism and began a gradual nationalization of U.S. petroleum holdings in Mexico. In complex fits and starts, Mexico's government insisted that it – not foreign firms – owned all sub-surface mineral rights (as per Spanish and Spanish colonial legal precedent). With billions of dollars at stake, U.S. oil companies sought special privileges, extra-territoriality, or in 1913-1914 and 1920-1921, U.S. military interventions on their behalf. Occupations of the chief Mexican port of Veracruz (1913) and of large portions of northern Mexico (1916-1917) did little to resolve disputes.[120]

---

119 The Mexican Revolution was four or five different revolutions interacting with each other. I got an appreciation of the whole via the careers of U.S.-based revolutionaries like Ricardo Flores Magon. See, i.e., Ward S. Albro, *Always a Rebel: Ricardo Flores Magon and the Mexican Revolution* (Fort Worth, Texas Christian University Press, 1992); Lowell L. Blaisdell, *The Desert Revolution: Baja California, 1911* (Madison,, University of Wisconsin, 1962); Chaz Bufe and Mitchell C. Verter (eds), *Dreams of Freedom: Ricardo Flores Magon Reader* (Oakland, California, AK Press, 2005) W. Dirk Raat, *Revoltosos: Mexico's Rebels in the United Sates 1903 1923* (College Station, Texas A & M Unversiity Press, 1985); Colin M. MacLachlan, *Anarchism and the Mexican Revolution: The Political Trials of Ricardo Flores Magon in the United States* (Berkeley, University of California Press, 1991).
120 Carleton Beals, *Mexican Maze* (Philadelphia, J. D. Lippincott, 1931), esp. Chapter 19 "Black Gold," pp. 333-51; Hans Schmidt, *Maverick Marine: General Smedley T. Butler and the Contradictions of American Military History* (Lexington, University Press of Kentucky, 1987). pp. 58-73.

As the political and economic winds started blowing against U.S. petroleum companies in Mexico after 1917, many started quietly switching their entrepreneurial attentions to Venezuela. By 1928, Gomez's satrapy had become the second-largest oil producing nation in the world after the U.S.A., surpassing Mexico. Dictator Juan Vicente Gomez ruled via the same mixture of domestic political repression and stability for external oil interests as Porfirio Diaz earlier had. Again like Diaz, Gomez kept his regime, police, spy system, and army robust with his share of fast-growing oil revenues. Gomez's Venezuela in the 1920's was Mexico without the Revolution, in any of its aspects. Gomez intended to keep it that way by threatening assassinations of foreign – and especially Mexican – leaders, if necessary.[121]

No love whatsoever, then, was lost between Mexican leaders trying to systematize a revolution and military tyrants like Gomez, who sought to smother any evidences of imported Mexican unions or "radicalism" they found. Puerto Rican socialist Santiago Iglesias accordingly made it clear to Munoz that Mexican money could help overthrow Gomez, the richest and best-protected of the Latin American tyrants, if a well-organized revolutionary force was ready to undertake the task.[122]

The Venezuelan Labor Union

Now Munoz had to devise a workable strategy to achieve this goal. Venezuelan exiles were often bitterly divided; a situation Gomez's always active spy service did nothing to decrease. Earlier "Garibaldian" efforts to invade Venezuela with small armies had repeatedly failed. Younger leftists like Munoz began to believe that organizing workers within Venezuela itself to serve as the internal foundation and springboard for revolution was far more important than trying to set the land ablaze via revolutionary vanguards

---

121 Thomas Rourke, *Gomez, Tyrant of the Andes* (New York, William Morrow, 1936-), i.e., pp. xv, 191.
122 Hanson, op. cit., p. 102.

operating outside the country. Munoz began by organizing a Venezuelan Labor Union in exile; then he sought to connect it to labor activists within the country via oilfield and refinery workers and sailors operating on ships regularly going to and from Venezuela. He met Mexican labor leader and cabinet officer Luis N. Morones in New York in 1924, outlined his strategy, and made his request for money and arms official. Morones, whose official responsibilities included overseeing Mexican military arsenals, was apparently encouraging. Now all Munoz needed was a real general for logistics, military training, and leadership.[123]

This is where Nogales came in. In him, Munoz got a genuine Ottoman army major who knew what he was about militarily. Nogales' political skills, however, lagged his military abilities. Nogales' letter of February 4, 1925, thanking the Venezuelan Labor Union for accepting him into membership, for example, first applauded the civic valor of the humble and the poor, as opposed to "aspiring caudillos" or venal intellectuals; but then it proceeded to argue that he had anticipated the organization's whole political program in 1911 and again in 1923. Overstating his earlier democratic devotions, Nogales almost made it sound as if Munoz's new Union was joining him.[124]

Grandiloquence like this had gotten Nogales in trouble before, and it did so again. Nogales headed to Mexico via Havana, Cuba, where he participated in the founding of the Anti-Imperialist League of the Americas in July. Meanwhile, Emilio Arevalo Cedeno, a former telegrapher who had repeatedly and unsuccessfully invaded Venezuela to overthrow Gomez, insured that he and his associates, not Munoz and Nogales, would enjoy the semi-official backing of the

123 Lluch-Velez, op. cit., pp. 219-21. This source's discussion of Nogales' activities is circumstantial and overstated. But it covers Venezuelan-Mexican governmental tensions well.

124 *Pensiamento Politico Venezolano del Siglo XX; Documentos para su Estudio; La Oposicion a la Dictatura Gomecista Vol. 4 Liberales Y Nacionalistas* (Caracas, Congreso de la Republica, 1983), pp. 159-60; De Trinca, op. cit., pp. 72-73.

Mexican government for a "Venezuelan Revolutionary Party" they created in Mexico City in 1926. In a scathing letter he wrote from Paris to an ally in Havana on November 24th, 1925, which Gomez's spies intercepted, Arevalo Cedeno bragged that he had already insured that the "hapless Nogales" was no longer representing the Venezuelan Labor Union (which Cedeno mockingly called the "Disunion") and that he had gotten Nogales "out of Mexico" as well. To Arevalo Cedeno, Nogales was a complete fraud. For all his military and other accomplishments, "there is no proof except for the mouth and audacity of that self-serving pleasure seeker." A few weeks earlier, ironically, Nogales had sent from Mexico another Gomez-intercepted letter to the same person Arevalo had addressed his own letter, thanking Arevalo Cedeno, whom Nogales had never met, for a favor and offering his friendship and alliance in return.[125]

Arevalo Cedeno was particularly notable for his sustained abuse of fellow Venezuelan exiles. Nogales' exaggerations (i.e. "General" Nogales), however, gave Arevalo's utter mistrust more traction than it otherwise might have had. Nogales, like Lawrence, was often his own worst enemy. In the case of the Mexican arms deal, additionally, Nogales had an older-fashioned habit of presenting a *carte d'visite* (visiting card) with a picture of himself on one side. The one he presented a Mexican official in 1926 was a slightly larger-than-normal version of himself as a Turkish cavalry officer; one of which he was then giving to "almost everybody he met" at occasions like the parties the Munoz Marin's put on in New York City.[126]

Nogales' self-advertisements, of course, could not compete with those of a Lowell Thomas theatrical extravaganza, but they nevertheless startled some and alienated others. Preceded by Arevalo Cedeno's crucial charges that he was a fraud, those charges now had unfortunate results: the offer of Mexican arms and funds was

---

125 De Trinca, op. cit., pp. 75-76.
126 Hanson, op. cit., p. 104.

suddenly withdrawn. When, years later, Munoz asked the Mexican official involved what had happened, the official heatedly replied:

"What happened?... What kind of a man did you send me? How am I going to have faith in a man who claims to be a world-famous general and who, on first meeting, shakes hands with one hand and shoves a picture postcard of himself at me with the other?"[127]

Affecting more grandeur than he had, then, Nogales only diminished his very genuine military accomplishments. Just as Field Marshal Allenby "always suspected a strong streak of the charlatan in Lawrence," so Nogales' compatriots among Venezuelan political exiles seem to have been un-nerved by his bouts of occasional megalomaniacal exhibitionism.[128]

The Path to Revolution in Nicaragua

The failure of Nogales' Venezuelan Labor Union effort with Munoz came about, in very large part, because of the ability of Gomez's spy service to uncover plots and create or heighten divisions among exile leaders. The Gomez dictatorship was nothing if not thorough in these regards. It regularly intercepted foreign mails between émigrés living outside Venezuela. Venezuelan ambassadors were responsible for keeping track of exiles abroad via networks of informers. Incoming newspapers, magazines, and suspect correspondence in all major languages were routinely read and censored in Venezuelan ports and post offices. By 1927, Gomez's huge intelligence apparatus accounted for just under fifteen percent of the annual national budget, totaling three and a half times more than all forms of educational spending. Gomez was an equal opportunity tyrant and spy, and his tastes in killing were utterly catholic. He imprisoned and murdered priests, poets, and peons alike for the slightest political opposition. The fate

---

127 Hansen, op cit., p. 104. See also, R. Norris Blake, "Nogales Mendez: Action was His Byword," *Revista Interamericana* (Puerto Rico), Vol. 7., (1977), pp. 547-57, esp. 552.
128 Wavell (1940), p. 193, as quoted in Stewart (1977). P, 171; De Trinca, p. 76.

of captured rebels was especially grisly. Opportunistic men of talent, however, whom Gomez mocked as "hombrecitos" – little men – made their peace with the regime and profited accordingly.[129]

At one point in 1926, following fifteen years of exile, Nogales himself may even have been tempted to seek a rapprochement with Gomez. Early in that year, the Venezuelan consul in Hamburg secretly reported home to Caracas that Nogales had approached him with an offer of cooperation with the Gomez regime, especially regarding the moribund Venezuelan Labor Union. Claiming not to have been involved in any invasion plot since 1914, Nogales asked for personal attention – and assurances of goodwill – from Gomez himself. What he got instead was additional attention from Venezuelan spies; detentions and arrests in Germany, Spain, and France; regular reports back home about his travels and non-involvements in Bolshevist plots; and finally a letter from Gomez himself to the Venezuelan ambassador in Berlin. The dictator expressed satisfaction with official reports attesting to Nogales' "insignificance" and his being "unbalanced with delusions of grandeur." "I also have the conviction," the Ambassador continued,

"…that his application for permission to return to the country is a farce, since he is well aware that no one will take him seriously, and, since he is not accustomed to work, he finds it easier to live abroad exploiting his position as an enemy of the government."[130]

There was clearly no place for Nogales in Gomez's happy land of "work, peace, and progress". Only five percent of Venezuelans there had ever had the franchise in the best of times. Sacrificing unknown political rights for specific economic advantages in an era of postwar boom and proliferating oil revenues was, therefore, initially comparatively easy. As long as the oil flowed, Gomez appeared politically unassailable.

---

129 Rourke, op. cit., pp. 133, 158-59, 293, 155-56, 137.
130 De Trinca, p. 79.

Nogales, meanwhile, was almost fifty years old at this time. Being thrown in prison in Spain in that year on the advice of the Venezuelan Minister – who said Nogales was a Bolshevik plotting revolution – and then being threatened with immediate deportation to Venezuela by Spanish authorities was not pleasant. Nor were other imprisonments and expulsion from Germany because his Venezuelan travel documents had again expired. Nogales affirmed his own strength and importance to his literary agent in New York, but by the middle of 1926, negotiations for a Spanish edition of *Four Years* had fallen through, he was tired, and the United States again looked like a good haven.[131]

Nogales, like many another political exile before and since, was deeply ambivalent about the United States. While admiring U.S. political institutions and ideals, he heartily disliked U.S. policies and actions in the part of the world he cared about the most. By 1927, there was much to dislike. Having seen a traditional old empire in the Middle East crumble, he now saw a new empire of "Dollar Diplomacy" rise in and around the Caribbean. In the decade since the opening of the Panama Canal in 1914, U.S. troops had been sent to Mexico, Nicaragua, Haiti, the Dominican Republic, Cuba, Panama, and Honduras, and were about to be sent back in larger numbers to deal with political unrest in Nicaragua. The Caribbean was an American lake and U.S. Presidents were policemen of the nations around it. Dollar diplomacy accepted, and profited from, thorough dictators like Gomez. He kept foreign investors happy and political stability absolute. Other Latin nations became battlegrounds.

Struggles were particularly bitter and bloody in the Dominican Republic and Nicaragua. Nicaragua's primary importance was geographical. It was the only other place in Central America where an inter-oceanic canal could easily be built. U.S. leaders overthrew Nicaraguan strongman Jose Santos Zelaya in 1909 for real and imaginary exercises of sovereignty. Included among these exercises

131 Nogales to Constance Skinner, April 6, 1926, Skinner Papers.

were hostile military moves against Honduras and El Salvador, contract disputes with a U.S. corporation with which then-Secretary of State Philander K. Knox was well connected, and rumored negotiations with Japanese and German representatives about selling rights to build a second canal not under American control. Once having overthrown Zelaya and his Liberal party, U.S. representatives backed a series of carefully selected Conservative rulers who rarely quarreled with U.S. dominance of Nicaraguan foreign and financial policy. The Bryan-Chamorro Treaty of 1914 demonstrated the degree to which Nicaragua had become a U.S. protectorate. For three million American dollars the United States bought a supposed monopoly grant to build a Nicaraguan canal: one that it never intended to use; but which excluded activity undertaken by any other nation.[132]

Meanwhile, small detachments of Marines were stationed in Nicaragua to help maintain stability. A major Liberal uprising was defeated in 1912. Ten smaller or larger rebellions occurred in the twelve years following. The standard and socially acceptable racisms of the day between all Caucasian U.S. Marines and mestizos, Indians, and Africans only added to the difficulties of the U.S. occupation. Most leaders of Zelaya's Liberal Party gradually accepted American domination of key elements of Nicaraguan sovereignty as a fact of political life. But the Liberal Party also pushed for honest elections which Conservative leaders had no interest in allowing. Efforts at political rapprochement between Liberal and Conservative parties were followed by a withdrawal of U.S. Marines, and an almost-immediate Conservative coup. Back came the Marines in 1922. The U.S. could neither abide nor risk replacing the brazen coup leader. So, after another four years of ineffective dither, another Liberal revolt began in earnest in 1926. To avoid further bloodshed, U.S. diplomatic leaders

---

132 Most of the money paid off Nicaraguan debts, and never left the United States. See i.e. Karl Hermann, *Under The Big Stick: Nicaragua and the United States Since 1848* (Boston, South End Press, 1986), pp, 170ff, 149ff.

now stage-managed the replacement of the Conservative who had led the coup with another Conservative long and exceedingly friendly to U.S. interests. New Conservative leader (and former clerk) Adolfo Diaz, however, impressed would-be U.S. kingmakers far more than Liberal rebels: who promptly conquered half the country and began marching on Managua, the Nicaraguan capital, "To put it vulgarly but accurately," the *New York Times* reporter on the scene later concluded, "in 1909 the United States took a bear by the tail, and it has never been able to let go." "Few things in its history," he ruefully added, "have brought more condemnation on the United States than has its career in Nicaragua."[133]

As Liberal rebels marched in for the kill against a weak and failing Diaz regime, U.S. President Coolidge sent a special envoy to Nicaragua to try and restore some credibility to American policy. Henry L. Stimson met with leading Liberal general Jose Maria Moncada and offered him a deal. The latest Conservative president maintained by U.S. power would stay in office briefly. Then the U.S. would oversee an honest-enough election that would (and did) elect Moncada. If he agreed and disarmed his troops as his mostly-beaten Conservative opponents did theirs, fine. If he did not, he and the Liberal party faced the threat of renewed U.S. military intervention, just as in 1912.[134]

Moncada took the deal Stimson offered. He shortly became Nicaragua's president. One of Moncada's generals, August Cesar Sandino, refused a U.S.-brokered and Marine enforced peace and began a six year guerilla war against Marine occupiers and their native allies. Sandino became one of the best-known leaders in Nicaraguan history.[135]

---

133 Harold Norman Denny, *Dollars for Bullets: The Story of American Rule in Nicaragua* (New York, Dial Press, 1929), p. 85.
134Henry L. Stimson, *American Policy in Nicaragua* (New York, Scribner's, 1927), p. 85
135 See, i.e. Neill Macaulay, *The Sandino Affair* (Chicago, Quadrangle, 1967).

Among Sandino's many Latin American supporters was Rafael De Nogales, to whom Henry Stimson was another in a long line of non-Spanish speaking Americans seeking to settle the affairs of societies he knew nothing about. Stimson, for example, reported that he was told that Sandino was a bandit who had lived in Mexico for twenty-two years, had served with Pancho Villa, and recruited a force composed mostly of "Honduran mercenaries" to engage in "violence and pillage." Stimson not only accepted such lies as truth, he put them in his memoir of his peacemaking mission to Nicaragua.[136]

Believing such nonsense, Stimson ignored nationalists like Sandino and helped lead the U.S. into a messy and brutal war that cost America heavily in terms of regional legitimacy, and which failed to accomplish a transition to a peaceful, multi-party democratic state in Nicaragua. Stimson's mistakes echoed down the decades. Anastasio Somoza, U.S.-educated and being fluent in English, very favorably impressed Stimson. Somoza also used a national police force the Americans helped him create to inaugurate a forty year family dictatorship of Nicaragua in 1936. Two years earlier, in 1934, Somoza had murdered Sandino, despite a previously signed peace treaty from 1933. A martyred Sandino in turn became the namesake of Marxist rebels, whose government U.S. President Ronald Reagan repeatedly tried to overthrow in the 1980s.

Henry L. Stimson and the aristocratic foreign policymakers who followed him understood little about the "underlying historical dynamics and the emotional climate" of Nicaraguan (or Latin American) politics. Instead, he saw power as a kind of elite jousting match among a set of "gentlemen politicians in Managua" and other national capitals. The job was then to pick "local auxiliaries" to maintain American interests. Alas for Nicaragua, the only two men that Stimson got hopelessly wrong, his most recent biographer concludes, "were the two [Sandino and Somoza] who would define the future of the country."[137]

---

136 Stimson (1927), p. 185.

Rafael De Nogales' pioneering critique of Stimson's Nicaragua policy, as we will see, often made more sense than the policies finalized by a man who very shortly became the Secretary of State for the United States of America during the presidency of Herbert Hoover. We shall also see, alas, that pioneering very often does not pay, in terms of either repute or income.

137 Godfrey Hodgson, *The Colonel: The Life and Wars of Henry Stimson, 1867-1950* (New York, Knopf, 1990), pp. 116-21, esp. 119.

Chapter Six

Nogales as a Critic of U.S. Imperialism

Rafael De Nogales' briefly high-profile, and now unknown, 1928 and 1931 criticisms of U.S. financial and military policies in Nicaragua were shaped by the "direct impact of political events," rather than by any cloistered ideology. In New York City in 1926, Nogales heard about increased U.S. intervention in Nicaragua. An acquaintance he met at the Newspaper Club in the city remarked that some of the same economic forces unable to control the social and economic changes in Mexico (to protect, i.e., U.S. petroleum investments) were now concentrating on smaller Central American nations like Nicaragua. Intrigued and interested, Nogales decided to investigate the Nicaraguan situation. With his war memoirs published in three languages and his efforts to overthrow Gomez via the Venezuelan Labor Union at an end, Nogales the man of action needed a project and Nogales the journalist needed an income. A Nicaraguan trip could satisfy both goals.[138]

Nogales, to repeat, was not a committed ideological leftist. "I have always felt great sympathies for the lefts," he wrote a close friend in October of 1929, "but I have never nor will ever be a left wing man myself. I would be acting against my nature and the traditions of my family if I did." Nogales' opposition to U.S. "Dollar Diplomacy" and military domination was primarily a nationalist protest against growing American intervention in Latin American affairs. American leaders simply did not have the right to restrict any Latin American nation's sovereignty to achieve their idea of a U.S.A. national mission. Caucasians, specifically, did not have a right to control the mostly indigenous or mestizo populations of Spanish America because of any

---

138 Nogales, *The Looting of Nicaragua* (New York, McBride and Company, 1928), pp. 43-44.

then-widely presumed Latin inferiorities in temperament or intellect.[139]

Moreover, Nogales believed that U.S. leaders regularly confused legitimate nationalist affirmations with illegitimate radicalism or Bolshevik revolution. Every Mexican reformist regime since the overthrow of Porfiro Diaz in 1910 had been branded inhumane, subversive, anticlerical, anti-capitalist – or all these and more besides. Nicaragua's situation was very similar. Astonishing ignorance had marched hand in hand with bad journalism, "one hundred per cent American," and "Make the Eagle Screech" arrogance, and a wonderful ability to clothe naked commercial interest in doctrines of disinterested nation building and liberty. If continued, such reactionary U.S. policies would needlessly alienate Latin American opinion. Further, they could easily, Nogales argued, create an international coalition against the United States. One composed, for example, of emerging Asian powers like Japan and China who saw Oriental exclusion immigration policies and other racist actions as offensive and aggressive. In World War I, Imperial Germany had learned the huge costs of swagger and conceits that alienated neighbors near and far. Imperial America could easily repeat Germany's experience.[140]

August Sandino, meanwhile, was anything but the mere bandit Moncada, Diaz, and others made him out to be to Henry Stimson. Most Nicaraguans supported Sandino's rebellion against U.S. occupation. Moreover, this was an age when the airplane and the

---

139 Rafael De Nogales to Constance Murray Skinner (from Mexico City), October 27, 1929, Skinner Papers, New York Public Library archives. For gentlemanly racisms of the era, see, i.e., Paul H. Beeker, Henry L. Stimson's *American Policy in Nicaragua the Lasting Legacy* (New York and Princeton, Markus Wiener, 1991. See also Ybarra, *Young Man of Caracas* for some witty summaries of the cultural norms of the period.

140 Nogales, *Looting of Nicaragua*, p. 47. The 1931 UK edition of this book had a new introduction emphasizing a "new world coalition" against the U.S.A. of Latin American and Asian powers, See esp. page 20.

machine gun had made aviation, not roving columns of Bedouin or other raiders, the master of the deserts and plains where guerilla horsemen had held sway for millennia. A new variety of guerilla leader was needed, one who could devise new tactics and strategies for a new age. Sandino, Nogales concluded, was this sort of new leader. As Nogales wrote in the English edition of his book:

> ...Sandino is neither a Napoleon nor a Hottentot, but... a born leader of men and a clever tactician, after the school of Abd el Krim of Morocco... Like Abd el Krim, Sandino succeeded in adapting modern military tactics to the topographic and climatic conditions of the region in which he is conducting his operations.[141]

Decades later, Sandino's first American biographer, a veteran of Fidel Castro's successful guerilla army, rightly called Sandino "one of the precursors of modern revolutionary guerilla warfare," and compared him favorably with China's Mao Tse Tung.[142]

In 1928, however, Nogales' military and political opinions strongly disputed those of the Republican administration of Calvin Coolidge, which, when it did not brand Sandino a bandit, branded him as a Bolshevik. They did so while protecting privileged elites from the prospects of sharing power with the great majority of their countrymen. Nogales' second book, *The Looting of Nicaragua*, was accordingly widely reviewed at a time when U.S. Marines were leading an anti-Sandino war. Analysts in places as varied as the *New York Times* and the *Hispanic American Historical Review* contrasted Henry L. Stimson's orderly, dispassionate, and uninformed views with Nogales' passionate, disorderly, and much better-informed analysis. Nogales' powerful indictment of U.S. Dollar Diplomacy and "big stick" military intervention, the reviewer for the *Journal of the Royal Institute of International Affairs* in London concluded, was

---

141 Nogales, *The Looting of Nicaragua* (London, Wright and Brown, 1931, p. 10.
142 Macaulay (1967). p. 9.

"one of the most outspoken condemnations of the Washington government and Wall Street interests ever put into print." It was also a "grave charge against a powerful administration in its dealings with a weak neighbor" that required consideration.[143]

Bitterness, disorganization, and a legal suit, however, deprived the original 1928 edition of Nogales' arraignment of U.S. policy in Nicaragua of much of its deserved effect. The bitterness came from Nogales' 25 years of political exile from his homeland and the bland arrogance and often breath-taking ignorance with which very highly regarded diplomats like Henry L. Stimson dealt with Latin American affairs. Stimson, who became Secretary of State in the Herbert Hoover administration of 1929 to 1933, seemed willing to accept almost any lies as truths if they promised uncomplicated regional economic and military advantage. Like fellow countryman, exile, and publicist Horacio Blanco Fambona, Venezuelan critic Nogales saw conservative U.S. leaders as bloody-handed hypocrites. Along with Senatorial critics of U.S. policy like Burton K. Wheeler and William H. Borah and left-wing readers of the *Nation* magazine, Nogales saw Sandino as a legitimate defender of Nicaragua's national sovereignty, and just the sort of strong-willed leader Latin America needed more of to replace dictators who were creatures of or sycophants to American power.[144]

143 Hodgson, *Stimson*, p. 111; Edgar Manning, review of Nogales' *The Looting of Nicaragua*, in the *Journal of the Royal Institute of International Affairs*, Vol. 7 (September, 1928), pp. 337-38. For other reviews, see, i.e., those by William MacDonald in the *New York Times*, (February 12,1928), p. 7; by Stewart Beach in *The Independent*, Vol. 120, March 3, 1928, p. 212; and Robert W. Dunn, in *The Nation*, Vol. 126, February 15, 1928, p. 188.
144 Miguel Jorrin and John D. Martz, *Latin-American Political Thought and Ideology* (Chapel Hill, University of North Carolina, 1970) pp. 392-93; Alfred Hasbrouck, review of Stimson, Nogales, and other books, *Hispanic American Historical Review*, vol. 9 (February, 1929, pp99-103, esp. pp. 102-03; Nogales, *Looting of Nicaragua*, pp. 157, 173.

Nogales, however, wrote his second book too angrily and too fast. So what he ended up with was what he himself once called a "potpourri" of observations and documents, more than a coherent narrative. It was as if decades of frustration boiled-over into furious digressions into how American policymakers had understood very, very little about Latin America since the Mexican Revolution of 1910. Stimson argued calmly, in a self-advertising "instant book", that he had taken the only reasonable and logical road there was to take. He sounded like exactly what he was: a successful Wall Street lawyer closing a business deal. Nogales' "instant book" counter-arguments often erupted in frustration at neat legalistic Stimson-like mind-sets that mixed ignorance and arrogance in a blender.

Nogales' reform proposals, when untangled from his passionate protests, were hardly revolutionary. They included removing corruption and ignorance among U.S. journalistic and diplomatic representatives in Latin America, making terms of loans and concessions revocable, withdrawing U.S. Marines, secularizing schools (along U.S. lines), limiting the political power of the Catholic clergy to get rid of the "Dark Ages substratum" of Latin politics, favoring competitive business over monopolies, and fostering Pan-American cooperation against the challenge of an "awakening Asia," which Nogales saw as the "great, probably the greatest, commercial power of the near future." Few Americans in the self-satisfied 1920s, however, thought they had anything significant to learn about Latin American – never mind Asian – affairs. Even fewer imagined that their country might appear regarding Nicaragua, as Germany had appeared when bullying and then invading a much smaller nation called Belgium in 1914.[145]

Another main reason Nogales' critique of U.S. policy failed to resonate was that the book was not widely or long available in the U.S.A. Nogales and his publisher quickly got embroiled in a then-gigantic $250,000 libel suit brought by a U.S. officer in 1929. One

145 Nogales, *Looting of Nicaragua*, pp. 295-99, 4-5, 63.

of Nogales' furious digressions in *The Looting of Nicaragua* involved the bloody excesses involved in U.S. suppression of a guerilla uprising in the Dominican Republic between 1916 and 1922. Fellow Venezuelan exile Horacio Blanco Fombona had witnessed and reported these events before being arrested and deported by U.S. military authorities. Nogales, who saw Blanco Fombona as "a political writer of no small importance," used lengthy extracts from Blanco Fombona's *Crimenes del imperialismo nordamericano* (Crimes of American Imperialism) published in Spanish in Mexico City in 1927. In this book, Blanco Fombona named names of men he saw as killers. A "Captain Taylor" of the U.S. Marines was among those listed and described.[146]

Later non-radical historians have used Blanco Fombona's sharp attack on U.S. policy and military practice as a credible source. Several officers other than Captain Taylor who Fombona mentioned by name had already become infamous. A later American academic analyst also concluded that legal recourse for those who had suffered mistreatment from the Marines or their Dominican police allies was effectively non-existent. Scandal and cover-up was only sufficient to cause Senate hearings in 1922 that documented large numbers of incidents of Marine violence against captured and suspected guerillas. Racist habits of mind among all white Marines unaccustomed to thinking of largely black Dominicans as equals were a key factor in human rights violations.[147]

Despite all of this, Nogales' newly-established publisher seems to have quickly withdrawn the book from circulation to avoid the risk

---

146 Nogales, *Looting of Nicaragua*, pp. 11, 268-69.
147 See, i.e., Bruce J. Calder, "Caudillos and Gavilleros versus the United States Marines: Guerilla Insurgency during the Dominican Intervention, 1916-1924, "*Hispanic American Historical Review*, Vol. 58 (November, 1978), pp. 649-75 is one of the very few recent treatments in English. See also: Sumner Welles, *Naboth's Vineyard: The Dominican Republic, 1844-1924* (two vols., New York, 1928), esp. chapters 8-15 and Melvin M. Knight, *The Americans in Santo Domingo* (New York, 1928).

of an expensive legal proceeding. Nogales, note, had not directly called the complaining Marine officer a war criminal himself; but instead had only quoted Fombona. Taylor, of course, could not sue non-resident Fombona or his Mexican publisher in a U.S. court, so he sued Nogales instead. Proving personal injury, however, generally requires that an author must *knowingly* use false material. This Nogales had not done. Blatantly rigged trials had imprisoned and deported socialists and anarchists in the U.S.A. for holding ideas deemed threatening to national security in the United States during wartime. But World War I and a postwar Red Scare were over. Nogales was also no leftist. The none-too-successful conspiracies he was involved in concerned the Gomez dictatorship in Venezuela, not the U.S.A. And, finally, the anti-guerilla war in the Dominican Republic he commented on in 1928 was 5 years or more in the past. Thus, Captain Taylor's ability to interweave his personal reputation with that of the government and nation he served was restricted.[148]

Nogales and his publisher, nevertheless, hardly reacted heroically, perhaps because of a stock market panic presaging the Great Depression that began in the same month as Captain Taylor's legal suit. Instead of defending free speech, each sought to shift all blame and financial responsibility upon the other. Nogales' new and probably undercapitalized publisher had wanted a "sensational book," and had signed a contract committing itself to bear half of any litigation expenses the book might generate. Nogales' literary agent further stated that she had advised both publisher and author to use pseudonyms for people charged with specific criminal acts. Both ignored her. The new publisher also, apparently, did not submit the book for a pre-publication legal review, as Nogales' agent also suggested. Nogales argued these omissions by the publisher relieved

148 For rigged trials, see, i.e. MacLachlan, op cit., pp. 76-92: For two classic treatments, see: Robert K. Murray, *Red Scare; A Study in National Hysteria, 1919-1921* (Minneapolis. Univ. of Minnesota, 1955) and William Preston, *Aliens and Dissenters: Federal Suppression of Radicals, 1903-1933* (Cambridge, Harvard. 1963).

him of all legal liability in the libel suit. His own personal knowledge of conditions in the Dominican Republic was so slight, meanwhile, that he asked the Dominican consul in New York to brief his lawyer on the subject.[149]

The upshot of everything was that Nogales' book was speedily withdrawn from circulation in the United States; probably as part of an out-of-court settlement by his frightened publisher with Captain Taylor. Nogales, notably, did not fight the libel case himself. His lack of citizenship rights and protections as a resident alien might well have inhibited Nogales from acting legally – as could a shortage of money. Survival, not heroism, was his operative principle.

Grandiloquence and megalomania, instead, quickly substituted for fact. Melodramatic stories excused Nogales' failure to act the part of the grand chivalric hero. In *The Looting of Nicaragua* libel case, as in the midst of the Armenian massacres fifteen years before, Nogales portrayed himself as being set-upon by herculean forces with topmost politico-military leaders in the nation out to ruin him. Instead of a single angry U.S. Marine Captain suing for an unusually large amount of money, intimidating the publisher, and thus halting the sales of a book, all of the forces of U.S. "Dollar Diplomacy" assembled had somehow conspired to perform the deed. Nogales penned legally irrelevant protests and promised the readers of a later and improved London edition of his book, explanations of the "Dollar Diplomacy"-supported libel suit – in an appendix – which he then never provided. Nogales, like his American publisher, avoided possibly-protracted legal proceedings neither could afford. "His was not a life of heroics," an American journalist who knew him later wrote, "just action."[150]

---

149 Rafael De Nogales to Field and Field attorneys, October 4, 1929; Nogales to Don Rafael Ortiz, October 1, 1929; Constance Lindsay Skinner to Nogales, September 28, 1929; and contract between Robert M. McBride and Company and Rafael De Nogales, August 12, 1927 – all in Box 7, Skinner Papers. New York Public Library Archives.

Myths and Realities

The Looting of Nicaragua, however, was not dead. A new and significantly improved edition of the book was published in London in 1931. Nogales had failed to get noted American anti-imperialist Senator William E. Borah of Idaho to write an introduction to the New York edition of 1927. But in the new London edition, Anti-imperialist Labour Party Member of Parliament Leonard W. Matters lauded Nogales' courage for penning a "damning indictment" of U.S. policy while only a resident alien in America. Matters knew something of such cross-cultural courage, as both a Parliamentary supporter of Mohandas Karamchand Gandhi and of Indian independence, and as an Australian Boer War veteran who was the London correspondent for *The Hindu*, one of India's most-important newspapers.[151]

Nogales' revised text removed almost all of the discussion of Fombona's charges about the Dominican Republic, removed an equally-discursive chapter on jungle travel in Nicaragua, erased some personal exaggerations, and added a new 20 page introduction about Nicaraguan politics which benefited from an interview with General August Sandino in Mexico City in 1929. Even with moderations, Nogales' new edition still flayed American diplomats for rampant hypocrisy and warned President Herbert C. Hoover, who was starting to withdraw Marine detachments in the wake of the onset of prolonged economic crisis at home, that the "crusted, hoary, ancient, cruel, ruthless, blind, insolent and lawless "Dollar Diplomacy," as

---

150 R. Norris Blake, "Nogales Mendez – Action Was His Byword," *Revista Intermaericana* [Puerto Rico], Vol. 7 (1977), p. 550; Nogales promised the explanation in a non-existent Appendix to the London edition of his book London, Wright and Brown, [1931] p. 8.

151 Senator William S. Borah to Rafael De Nogales, October 14, 1927, Skinner Papers. Nogales, *Looting of Nicaragua* (1931 ed.), pp. vii-viii. For Matters, see: *Who's Who* (London, A and C Black, 1932); the obituary in *The Hindu* for November 2, 1951 and his second book, *Through the Kara Sea: A Narrative of a Voyage in a Tramp Steamer Through Arctic Waters to the Yenisei River* (London, Skeffington and Son, [1932]).

managed by Wall Street bankers, was as politically dangerous as ever.[152]

The era of Nogales' strenuous political involvements, however, was also now fast coming to an end. His trip to Nicaragua in 1927 had involved difficult overland and river travel through a sparsely-settled region of a country in the midst of a civil war. Given that Nogales was then fifty years old, bodily penalties were inevitable. His included a bad lung infection, a severe tear in the stomach muscles, and an abscess on the liver or spleen due to jungle fever. The latter required a major surgical operation in Germany. One of Nogales' longtime physician friends subsequently advised greatly reduced physical activity to avoid further surgical risks.[153]

Nogales was clearly in a mood to accept such medical advice. Two of his letters of February, 1928 to his literary agent show an angry and exhausted man railing at all-too-common advertising carelessness by his U.S. publisher (in-advance of the libel suit). They also show a man anxious about his physical and mental health, and melodramatically talking about suffering "another nervous breakdown" and becoming "a useless wretch for the rest of my life." His agent was especially criticized for marketing copy that mangled and exaggerated Nogales' military experience and rank, and which threatened to brand him a "a 'braggart' and a 'fake'" to British journalists and German and other officers. It did not help, however, that Nogales blamed his agent for making him appear to be a "laughing stock" while, at the same time, falsely claiming to have achieved the rank of general (as opposed to major) in the Ottoman army. Yet again in life, Nogales was becoming his own worst enemy.[154]

Simultaneously, Nogales was carefully avoiding mentioning Dictator Juan Vicente Gomez or Venezuela at all. Nothing about the

---

152 Nogales, *Looting of Nicaragua* (1931), p. 3.
153 "De Nogales Operated On," *New York Times*, March 15, 1928, p. 8; Nogales to Skinner, May 30, 1928 (from London), Skinner Papers.
154 Nogales to Skinner, February 23, 1928 and February 21,1928, Skinner Papers.

events he discussed in Nicaragua was ever directly connected to Venezuela in any way. Nogales may well have wished to avoid the harassments he'd suffered in connection with *Four Years*. Whatever the case, he was notably cautious. The same caution applied to his part-Indian heritage: which Nogales also wanted kept very private. [155]

Caution may have marched hand-in-hand with Nogales' desire to reinvent himself. His first two books treated his personal involvements in dramatic and important events. He had, in the process, become something of a New York literary celebrity. Reporters there regularly sought him out as a commentator on the latest Venezuelan insurrection or Central American coup. He featured regularly in the columns of the *New York Times*. *Time* only half jokingly referred to him as "the self appointed paramount chief of Venezuelan revolutionists."[156]

Nogales' name even shone in fiction. His literary agent, Constance Lindsay Skinner, wrote well regarded and successful adventure novels for adolescent boys and girls. In 1927, her often reprinted *The Tiger Who Walks Alone* appeared. The book not only reprised Nogales' life, it was dedicated to him and had a frontispiece depicting him as well. In literature, if not in life, Nogales fought off bandits and criminals, quick-changed into a dress suit, tamed unspeakable Turks, charmed audiences over dinner, and then led "his people to liberty over jungle and pampas" without a hitch, finally destroying the evil dictator of a fictional Latin American land with ...an airplane. Complimented both for its lack of racial superiority, its unusual Latin theme, and for the attractive and exciting nature of its main character in journals like

---

155 Nogales to Skinner, November 21, [1927], "Off Boulogne sur Mer," Skinner Papers.
156 "Falke Filibuster," *Time*, August 26, 1929, at: www.time.com/ magazine (accessed 1/23/2007); Morris Gilbert, "Venezuela Menaced by Shadow of Revolt," *New York Times*, August 25, 1929, p. 18; "Venezuelan Rebels Appeal to Holland," *New York Times*, July 1, 1929, p. 52; "Dictator Puts 25 Women Foes in Crazy House," *Chicago Daily Tribune*, March 27, 1929, p. 27.

The New Republic and the *Nation*, and in newspapers including the *New York Herald Tribune*. The popularity of *The Tiger Who Walks Alone* also clearly demonstrated Nogales' salability to wider readerships than those concerned with Armenian massacres or U.S.-led anti-guerilla wars in Nicaragua.[157]

Nogales Reinvents Himself

Nogales quickly appreciated that he had exotic celebrity. In an era when fewer than one per cent of adult Americans had a college degree or had travelled abroad, a Latin revolutionary who had fought for the Turks and then gone in search of guerilla chieftains in Nicaraguan jungles possessed a small part of the same mysterious and romantic flavor that had already turned "Lawrence of Arabia" into one of the major media-built celebrities of the modern age.

The problem now became how to tell the tale of Nogales' early life previous to the First World War. At issue, as so often before, was how much myth to interweave with exciting and unusual realities. Nogales had done things like mine for gold in Alaska, sell speculative properties during a silver boom in Nevada, and work as a cowboy along the Rio Grande. But he also exaggerated his tales about these experiences in ways not unlike Lawrence. He also made other claims about his early youth for which he was – and remains – the only known source, and which researchers from his native land have yet to be able to confirm. In creating a past for himself, then, Rafael De Nogales mixed History with Hollywood, and life with movie.

We can see the process at work in a letter Nogales wrote to his agent in November of 1927. In February of that year, Joseph Bushnell Ames, a writer of Western novels, was reported to be at work on Nogales' "recollections of his early experiences as a cow-puncher

---

157 Constance Murray Skinner, *The Tiger Who Walks Alone* (New York, Macmillan, 1927), see esp. "Author's Note", p. 211, Dedication, and Frontispiece (modeled on Nogales). For reviews, see, i.e., *The New Republic* (November 16, 1927), p. 362; the *Nation*, (November 16, 1927), p. 552; *New York Herald Tribune*, November 20, 1927, p. 8.

in the west." Ames was then succeeded by a not-further identified ghostwriter named "Allen." Allen then apparently followed agent Constance Skinner's advice to "write short … sentences intermingled with philosophical discussions, etc., and to pay little attention to scenery…" This, Nogales complained to Skinner, was "just the contrary of what he intended." Allen, Nogales elaborated, had "filled the first thirty thousand words [of his manuscript] with a flood of empty words…" Nogales told Skinner to "read over the scenario I left you and tell him to cut all that stuff out and keep strictly to the way I laid the plot down." Dancehall fights, for example, could be "cut down to a few sentences. He does not need pages to describe them. As a novel, all that superfluous stuff becomes tiresome, and for the *motion picture* screen all that stuff is not necessary." (Italics mine)[158]

"Action and scenery," Nogales continued, "is what people want." Instead of "private opinions," they wanted "short and picturesque scenes and a touch of poetry." Nogales had left a "synopsis" of plot and characters for his experiences in Alaska, Nevada, and elsewhere. The ghostwriter should just stretch out that synopsis "as it stands, adding a couple or three new characters to it." This would produce a successful book. The current beginning should be scrapped, "philosophical slush and empty words" should be thrown out, and writing should be "short and to the point." "I wish also to insist," Nogales closed, "that my family or family names – as well as Venezuela – be left out of that (sic) story." Family and descent issues would not be discussed "now and forever."[159]

Nogales, therefore, very clearly wanted an autobiography-based action novel that told much of what he had done, and very little indeed about who he was or what his motives were. He also, and as clearly, wanted a plot-line suitable for movie-makers who would

---

158 Nogales to Constance Skinner, November 2, [1927], Skinner Papers. (See also a clipping from the *Lynchburg News* [Virginia] dated February 13, 1927 in the same collection).
159 ibid.

likely rework characters and scenes, as he said, "to suit themselves anyway." "The less [personal or philosophical] detail, the better for them," Nogales concluded.[160]

Nogales, here, placed unusual degrees of responsibility on his agent, and also paid her an unusually-large one-third share of his total royalties for her efforts. He was also clearly conscious of the popularity of successful romantic movie epics of the mid-1920s like "The Sheikh" and "The Son of the Sheikh" featuring Hollywood star Rudolph Valentino. Men like Lawrence (with a large assist from Lowell Thomas) had popularized exotic Islamic locales. The first movie rights of the only book ever made widely available in his lifetime, Lawrence's *Revolt in the Desert*, were purchased by filmmaker Alexander Korda from Lawrence shortly after his book appeared in 1927. The exotic aristocrat off doing unusual things in the sun and sand was a staple of 1920's and 1930's adventure romances. Nogales could not compete with the robed savior of the British Empire, the Holy City of Jerusalem, and Western Civilization charging into history amidst crowds of dashing Bedouin. Nogales, however, hoped to get his piece of the romantic action with his cowboy and gold and silver rush experiences in the U.S.A. in the years from 1900 to 1910.[161]

No memoir or novelization of Nogales' western adventures, however, was ever completed. The ghost-writer gave up, and Nogales did not – for the moment – do the job himself. Nor did Nogales' subsequent effort to write what a *New York Times* reporter said was an historical romance with a "Near East setting" get anywhere. Instead, Nogales fell back on journalism to pay the bills.[162]

---

160 ibid.
161 For the influence of Lawrence on Hollywood, see., i.e., Hodson, op. cit., pp. 65-71 and Crawford, op. cit, pp. 145-46. Today, an established agent who simply sells a book and negotiates a contract with a commercial publisher generally gets 10 to 15 percent of the royalties and the author's advance (against later royalties).

Here, he enjoyed some substantial success. Much of his writing from the late 1920s has yet to be discovered, but occasional examples give a sense of a writer whose status as a commentator on events in Latin America and the Middle East was slowly growing. In 1928, he was first approached by *Critica*, a Buenos Aires newspaper, about serial publication of a Spanish translation of his book on Nicaragua. Noted leftist analyst of Latin America Carleton Beals thought this book "remarkable." Nogales placed stories in Joseph Pulitzer's *New York World* on Palestine, Mexico, and a proposal for a United States of Europe in 1929. That same year, he interviewed August Sandino while in Mexico City to report on that country's elections. Further reporting about Central American events followed, and Nogales began to be interviewed by radio commentators in the United States.[163]

Nogales' feature article in the *Washington Post* of September 8, 1929 was another step up the journalistic ladder. For the topic of this long and well-advertised feature essay was petroleum politics in the Middle East. World War 1 had demonstrated the crucial importance of oil to national security. Post-war military mechanization only underwrote the point that great powers without secure access to oil supplies were very vulnerable.[164]

Both Britain and France, Nogales argued in his *Washington Post* essay, would stop at nothing to control a vital resource. U.S. firms were being frozen out of control over Iraqi oilfields as they had earlier

---

162   For the "Zobeida the Pearl of the Orient" novel, see: *New York Times*, March 31, 1931, p. 52 and De Trinca, op. cit., pp. 83, 103.

163   Nogales to Skinner, May 30, 1928 and October 27, 1929 (from Mexico City), Skinner Papers; Carleton Beals, *Glass Houses: Ten Years of Free Lancing* (Philadelphia, Lippincott, 1938). Beals did not, however, mention Nogales' earlier work on Nicaragua in his book on Nicaragua and August Sandino, *Banana Gold* (Philadelphia, Lippincott, 1932), even though he had met Nogales, en route to Mexico by ship, in 1929 and knew of his Nicaragua book.

164   Daniel Yergin, *The Prize: The Epic Quest for Oil, Money, and Power* (New York, Simon and Schuster, 1991) is a good introduction.

been excluded from Iranian oil fields. Britain and France would also sacrifice the human rights of any regional ethnic or religious group which threatened control of petroleum reserves or strategic pipeline routes to Mediterranean ports. The British would sacrifice the Zionist Jews of Palestine as quickly as the French would sacrifice the Maronite Christians of Lebanon – and as both had squelched the interests of Armenians trying to lay claim to eastern provinces of the former Ottoman Empire. Ideals meant very little when interests came into play. The British had already sacrificed Feisal's kingdom in Syria, one that he and T. E. Lawrence had labored especially hard to create during and after the Arab Revolt, to preserve Britain's relations with France. Britain later installed Feisal as monarch in Iraq as a consolation prize. In any contest between majority Muslims and religious minorities, Muslims would win-out: Because upon them primarily depended the safety and security of prospective oil pipelines and railways.[165]

Nogales, like pioneering contemporary oil analyst Ludwell Denny, clearly believed that imperialism and regional oil dominance marched hand in hand. Major powers expanded into oil-rich regions possessing weak and vulnerable governments offering political, economic, or military favors. If local warlords, like Venezuela's Juan Vicente Gomez, then helped keep the oil flowing through U.S.-built pipelines from U.S.-drilled wells, that was all that was required. Issues of popular freedoms or human rights were secondary. The U.S. government and American oil firms jockeyed Britain out of the oil fields of the Caribbean to assure regional economic, military, and political dominance – just as Britain jockeyed U.S. firms out of Iran and Iraq for the same reasons. These global oil struggles happened with particular force because 1920's U.S. oilmen incorrectly believed their domestic reserves of petroleum were fast running out.[166]

---

165 Rafael De Nogales, "Control of Oil Fields in Western Asia Revives Strife in Palestine and Syria... England Seen Stopping at Nothing to Retain Fuel for Navy," *Washington Post*, September 8, 1929.

The influence of oil also had prominent domestic dimensions. Charles Evans Hughes, former New York governor and Republican presidential nominee in 1916, illustrated this. Hughes, like Stimson, was a Wall Street lawyer. He was Secretary of State from 1921 to 1925, as "Dollar Diplomacy" became a more prominent and more debated aspect of U.S. Latin American policy. He then became the counsel for the American Petroleum Institute and the Standard Oil Company of New Jersey (now EXXON) for several years before returning to Washington as Chief Justice of the United States Supreme Court in 1930.[167]

Nogales as "Radical"

Oil's importance in America's domestic and foreign affairs only further complicated Nogales' life in America. Above all things, Nogales believed in national sovereignty. Big nations did not have a right to tell smaller nations in their sphere of interest what to do. Nor did they have the right to create or prop-up dictatorial puppet-regimes to do their bidding. Nogales the Venezuelan nationalist opposed U.S. efforts in Nicaragua on the basis of actions, not theory. U.S. leaders simply had no right to limit Nicaraguan independence in key matters like building another inter-oceanic canal. Nor did they have the right to send U.S. Marines to support those who agreed to rule within their mandates. General August Sandino was a hero because he fought for his country when others merely maneuvered for affluence or office. That Venezuelan or Nicaraguan or Mexican politics were imperfect was not the point. The point was that it was up to Venezuelans or Nicaraguans to resolve their problems. A non-Marxist Mexican Revolution had demonstrated the process was already underway. The U.S. should now stand aside rather than to try and police the hemisphere.

---

166 Ludwell Denny, *We Fight For Oil* (New York and London, Knopf, 1928), esp. pp. 17-18.
167 Denny, p. 20.

Ideas like this were easy for the complacent or the conservative to confuse with Bolshevism, especially if they were those numerous Americans who generally considered Latin Americans as both racially and culturally inferior. As racism – either as active hatred or dislike or as bland assumptions of universal superiority – was widespread in the U.S.A., mixed-race Rafael De Nogales had seen his share of it. As early as 1909, in a letter to a Caracas newspaper proposing Japan as a counterweight to U.S. power in Latin America and the Caribbean, Nogales had remarked that racism was nothing less than an "inner gangrene" silently infecting and undermining the strength and unity of the United States.[168]

The gentlemen travelers of the Explorer's Club of New York seem to have had little active contempt for Rafael De Nogales in December of 1930. Senses of universal superiority towards fiery and illogical Latins, however, were hardly absent. Given this, any strongly-expressed dislike for U.S. oil interests whose royalties underwrote the Gomez dictatorship could easily be seen as equivalent to Red revolution.

Such fears were ironic given Nogales' often-demonstrated ability to charm educated people of property and intellectual standing. Places like the Explorer's Club were important to Nogales. In numerous ways he was an independent journalist and writer often looking for work. Prestigious gathering places like it provided locales where writers, explorers, scholars, benefactors, corporate sponsors, and journalists all met. In this "motley but polite exploring milieu," travelers would raise money for expeditions, network, find new jobs, and self-advertise, all this in an era preceding modern state-funded scientific or other research. Nogales, additionally, lived in a room at

---

168 Rafael De Nogales, *Verdades: Serie de Articulos Economico-Politicos publicados en Caracas durante el ano 1909 Gral Rafael de Nogales Mendez* (Caracas, 1909), pp. 8-9 (This very rare pamphlet is available in only a single copy located in the Collection Arcaya of the National Library of Venezuela. Many thanks to Mirela Quero De Trinca for a copy of this source).

the Explorer's Club at this point in his career. So he decided to apply for membership in the club as someone who had engaged in exploration and added to the sum of geographic knowledge. Nogales had already become associated with the American Geographical Society of New York (a competitor to the better-known and more successful National Geographic Society), the Royal Geographical Society, and a German equivalent. A further membership, he hoped, would gain him credibility and support as a traveler, journalist, and writer.[169]

In a post World War I era when Walter Lippmann could write that areas like Russia, the Balkans, Turkey, and Africa were "lands intellectually practically unexplored" and when those who had investigated the interiors of countries like Nicaragua or Venezuela numbered in the very small handfuls, Nogales' application made sense. He was multi-lingual, experienced, widely traveled, twice-published and well-reviewed. A global depression was also well underway. So Nogales may have needed all the additional status, connections, and employment opportunities he could get.[170]

Unfortunately, Nogales was still quite capable of angering conservatives. This was clear after two liberal members, Icelandic-Canadian Arctic explorer Vilhjalmur Stefansson and Luis Munoz Marin and Muna Lee's friend Earl Parker Hanson, nominated Nogales to Explorer's Club membership in December of 1930. Though Stefansson was particularly impressed with Nogales' knowledge of sub-Arctic environments (which he had gained as a gold miner and surveyor around present-day Fairbanks, Alaska in 1904-1905), three other club members, all businessmen, were anything but impressed with Nogales' remarks on tropical locales.[171]

169 Neil Smith, *American Empire: Roosevelt's Geographer and the Prelude to Globalization* (Berkeley, University of California Press, 2003), pp. 198-200.
170 ibid., p. 111 (Lippmann to Secretary of War Newton D. Baker, in May, 1918. As U.S. leaders were trying to apply Woodrow Wilson's universal principles of sovereignty and national self-determination to lands few knew very much about.

The first of the critics said that he had "heard a lot about" Nogales in Venezuela. He was "an openly avowed and fanatical enemy of, and conspirator against, a friendly government ... in which several of our fellow-members have interests." Moreover he was issuing tirades against U.S. oil companies, the U.S. generally, and threatening to burn all the oil wells and towns of Venezuela if any foreign power landed troops to protect the interests of their nationals.[172]

The next businessman member opposed to Nogales' candidacy made precisely the same points. Nogales was an "Anti-American" clearly plotting revolution and would destroy "all property owned by Americans ... especially the Oil Interests." This person did not believe Nogales had a large following in Venezuela or much influence there. So, "the threat of what he intends to do cannot be taken very seriously, but it is offensive to many members ... to hear that kind of talk in the Club rooms." Unless the Explorer's Club wanted to be used as a cover for "the headquarters of a Revolutionary Junta," Nogales' application should be refused.[173]

The third and final opponent also chimed-in that he, too, had heard that Nogales intended bloody revolution; after which "one of his first acts will be to destroy all property of the various American companies, especially if the government should make any protest on their behalf."[174]

"So many disgruntled and exiled Venezuelans, of much more prominence than Mr. De Nogales," this member continued,

---

171 Vilhjalmur Stefansson to membership committee, November (sic) 13, 1930; Earl Hanson to Membership Committee, December 8, 1930, "Rafael De Nogales" file, Explorer's Club Archives, New York, New York.
172 William C. Kaelin to Membership Committee, December 12, 1930, Explorer's Club Archives.
173 M. J. Bolan to Membership Committee, December 17, 1930, Explorer's Club Archives.
174 C. V. Wells to Membership Committee, December 11, 1930, Explorer's Club Archives.

have, during the past twenty years [of Gomez's dictatorship] from safe distances like New York, Curacao, and Trinidad, announced, in advance, that they were about to overthrow the Venezuelan government, that their 'mouthings' are not now taken very seriously. But I do not recall that any of them has threatened to destroy the property of Americans "if and when" he should seize the reins of government.

An "adventurer of this type," the third businessman orated, should not even be allowed a room in the Explorer's Club, never mind membership. Letters like this served their purpose. Nogales' election was cancelled and his application for membership was refused.[175]

---

175   ibid.

Chapter Seven

The End of Rebellion

Ironically, just as three businessmen with contacts and markets in
Venezuela who were all members of the exclusive Explorer's Club of
New York argued that Rafael De Nogales was an incendiary radical,
his days of war and revolution were fast coming to an end. Four
factors were especially important here. First, in Venezuela itself, a new
political generation, the "Generation of 1928," had arisen among the
tiny minority of only several hundred existing university students in
the country. This new generation's educated elite thought far more in
terms of building political parties within Venezuela than in terms of
altering the country via invasions and raids from without. Second, the
failure of the well-planned "Falke" seaborne raid of 1929
demonstrated the vainness of expecting continued external attacks to
transform a country that many of the anti-Gomez exiles like Rafael
De Nogales had not lived in for twenty years and more. This was,
additionally, almost as long as reform-minded young students of the
"Generation of 1928" like Romulo Betancourt had been alive. Third,
to the forces of generational change and alterations in basic political
strategy were added the continuing inability of Nogales and other
older exiles to avoid having their conspiratorial networks penetrated
by Gomez's well-paid and numerous spy service. Fourth and finally,
there was an aging Nogales' necessity of earning a living by writing,
in a Depression Decade, when it was difficult to get financial support
for creative work of any kind.

Venezuela's "Generation of 1928" was the hinge on which
everything else turned. Juan Vicente Gomez, probably illiterate
himself, cared little for educating others. A diversifying and growing
economy, however, needed "hombrecitos" who would do Gomez's
specialized bidding. Members of this tiny educated elite like law
student Romulo Betancourt were born in 1908, the year that Gomez

seized power in Venezuela. They could remember no other leader than "El Benemerito" (The Well-Deserving). Gomez's dictatorship was not generally well-known outside Venezuela and its savagery was well veiled. Venezuela, much as its regime kept a very low profile, also was the Saudi Arabia of the 1920's, and the second-largest oil-producing nation in the world by 1928. Waves of cash from foreign petroleum companies helped Gomez guarantee peace and increase prosperity in a land he viewed, in all essential respects, as his personal property.[176]

All was not well, however, on Gomez's nation-wide hacienda. Gomez had controlled local warlords and brought the landowning elite into an alliance of convenience with the regime. The Venezuelan government budget, fueled by oil revenues, rose 20 times from 1922 to 1935 alone. Gomez, however, had to pay for the personalized way he managed Venezuela's most valuable resource. He and his family benefitted greatly from special petroleum deals. Venezuelan oil, however, also sold for 1/3 less than Mexican. Gomez clearly offered U.S. oilmen better deals than they could get in either Mexico or the Middle East. The significant measures of toleration and protection as a "friendly regime" that he enjoyed, in foreign business and governmental circles, accordingly, did not come free.[177]

Younger Venezuelans like Betancourt who could not remember the era of caudillos and thorough political gangsterism that preceded Gomez, however, took things like dictatorial stability and increasing economic standards as a given. To them, Gomez was just another Porfirio Diaz of Mexico: a corrupt dictator profiting from selling

176 Thomas Rourke, *Gomez, Tyrant of the Andes* (New York, William Morrow, 1936), pp. 189-91. B. S McBeth, *Juan Vicente Gomez and the Oil Companies in Venezuela, 1908-1935* (Cambridge, Cambridge Univ. Press, 1983). pp. 14, 70.
177 Gomez was regularly "invited" to invest as a shareholder in oil companies operating in Venezuela. He also created his own personal oil company and used oil concessions to "secure political loyalty and to reward faithful government officials." McBeth, op cit,. pp. 71, 76, 83, 96.

control over key aspects of the economy to foreigners. "A Republic For Sale," Romulo Betancourt later titled the first section of a book on oil and politics in Venezuela he began writing in the 1930s and which was first published in Spanish in the 1950s. Simply put, the Venezuela Betancourt knew seemed entirely a creation of Gomez; and Gomez, to young members of the Generation of 1928 like Betancourt, was almost entirely a flawed creation of foreign diplomats, navies, and intelligence services. Laden with foreign decorations, "El Benemerito" presided over a country with wild income and wealth inequalities. Two-thirds of the population was illiterate. Only 18 high schools, 532 university students and 60 teachers with advanced degrees existed in a nation of over 3 million people.[178]

Normally, a warlord who had created Venezuela's first centralized state and used contracts with foreign oil firms to do it might have cared little about protests from a few score university students in Caracas. But their calls for national reform in 1928 also produced unexpected and widespread popular support and even a brief and unsuccessful military uprising of junior officers in the Venezuelan army. The combined result of all this produced immediate and sharp repression. Those that escaped indefinite prison terms or assignments to work building roads provided a new group of already-numerous Venezuelan political exiles.[179]

This new generation of Venezuelan political exiles, moreover, had some significant differences from the old. They were better educated. They tended to scatter to Latin America, not Europe or the U.S. They also had more of an appreciation of the necessity of popular support and popular political organizations as agents for change. Just as these young people had grown into adulthood with Juan Vicente Gomez's

178 Romulo Betancourt, *Venezuela: Oil and Politics* (Boston, Houghton Mifflin, 1979 (first English edition)), pp. 3-48, esp. 10-11, 49.
179 John D. Martz., "Venezuela's 'Generation of '28': The Genesis of Political Democracy," *Journal of Inter-American Studies*, Vol. 6 (January, 1964.), pp. 17-32, esp. 18-20.

dictatorship, they had also grown into adulthood with the models of the Mexican and Russian Revolutions mobilizing masses.[180]

This also meant that the young Romulo Betancourt, a major leader of the new Venezuela of the future, more closely resembled a younger Luis Munoz Marin than he did an older Rafael De Nogales. When Munoz had sought to combine older-style revolutionary invasion with newer style Mexican labor and popular organization in 1926, he had sent Nogales to try and raise money from a founder of the Mexican organized labor movement and a national leader in a political party which had elected two Mexican presidents. Nogales was to lead the troops of an ill-starred and spy-infested "Venezuelan Labor Union." The organization, however, was meant to be far different than the traditionalist following of an Andean regional caudillo. Instead of making revolution by merely defeating the other man at the top, the new approach emphasized creating political parties active at all levels of society. Rather than merely creating insurrections, issuing pronouncements, and then believing that top-down political transformation could occur by fiat, the new approach emphasized ongoing negotiations within permanent organizations.[181]

As one result of this generational change, Betancourt was in contact with the older "caudillo" exiles like Nogales only briefly after Betancourt's own exile in 1928. Though Betancourt apparently took part in one small invasion attempt in 1929 that never even reached Venezuela, he had also apparently given-up on top-down armed insurrections by the end of that year.[182]

A particular reason for newer exiles like Betancourt's disenchantment with the insurrectionary approach was the failure of

180 ibid, p. 18.

181 For Luis Napoleon Morones, the Mexican labor and political leader whose influence was dominant in the 1920s, see: J. H. Retinger, *Morones of Mexico A History of the Labour Movement in that Country* (London, Labour Publishing Company Inc., 1926 — republished in a limited edition of 100 by Documentary Publications, Washington DC, 1976).

the best-planned and equipped external invasion of Venezuela ever undertaken during Gomez's 28 year long reign. In August of 1929, a German ship called the "Falke" loaded 125 armed Venezuelan exiles in Poland, outside of the reach of Gomez's well-established ambassadorial spy networks in Western Europe. Under the command of General Romano Delgado Chalbaud, an exiled former chief of the Venezuelan navy, the group was to stage a surprise attack against Cumana, a large port in eastern Venezuela with a well-supplied arsenal.

When the "Falke" raid began, a bloody battle ensued between Chalbaud's troops and those of the defending garrison. Both Chalbaud and the opposing commander were soon killed. So were enough other invading officers and men to cause a retreat from the beach — especially after a government airplane flew overhead, raking the landed rebels with bombs and machine guns. Chalbaud's surviving son and men quickly steamed off to seek — and obtain — political refuge in Trinidad.[183]

Interviewed by *Time* magazine about the raid, Rafael De Nogales frankly admitted that he and other "old established opponents of the dictator Gomez" had not backed Chalbaud's effort, believing it some effort to regain Gomez's favor by betraying his associates. "Last week," *Time* continued, "Rafael de Nogales, self-appointed paramount chief of Venezuelan revolutionists, boasted that he thought the Falke filibuster was really an attempt by the suspect participants to prove to him how much in earnest they really are."[184]

182 *The Antologia Politica de Romulo Betancourt* is a multi-volume chronological series that the Editorial Fundacion de Romulo Betancourt began publishing in Caracas, Venezuela in 1990. There are currently six volumes of all known Betancourt correspondence, memos, and reports. My data on Betancourt's relationship with Nogales and the others of the "caudillo" generation comes from Mirela Quero De Trinca, the editoress of Volume 6 of the collected series, (De Trinca to author, March 16, 2008.
183 Rourke, op. cit., pp. 238-49, esp. 243-48; "Falke Filibuster", *Time*, August 26, 1929. (from www.time.com/magazine — accessed 1/ 23/ 2007).

In this latter bit of thoughtless megalomania, Nogales demonstrated exactly the negative qualities that he had so passionately accused General Jose Manuel (Mocho) Hernandez of possessing as a self-styled "Young Turk" sixteen years before. Only now it was he who was waging rebellion from quarters in New York. Now it was Nogales who was unaware of the changed realities of their homeland.[185]

Inventing a Past

Nogales' grandiosity to a *Time* reporter, fortunately, was hardly the only commentary he made on events in Venezuela. The *New York Times* and *Chicago Daily Tribune*, among others, continued to use him as a reliable source on rebellions and unrest. His knowledge, however, was increasingly dated. The Venezuela he had known was changing. Moreover, in October of 1929, a deep and decade-long world-wide depression began which spared only a few suppliers of essential raw materials (among which was oil-rich Venezuela). An expatriate Nogales had to make a living in a challenging economic environment. That inevitably meant journalism. Magazines and newspapers, however, saw their subscriptions decline with readers' incomes. Placing stories got harder and the buyers paid less. For a free-lance political writer like Nogales, finding popular new things to write about Latin America after Mexico's politics stabilized and U.S. Marines withdrew from Nicaragua in 1932 was not going to be easy.[186]

---

184 "Falke Filibuster," *Time*, August 26, 1929.

185 Sadly, in his fourth and final book, published only in the United Kingdom, Nogales used the Falke raid, suitably disguised, as one of the tales of things *he* had done in *his* own life. See: *Silk Hat and Spurs*, (London, Wright and Brown, [1934], pp. 57-72.

186 "Venezuelan Rebels Appeal to Holland," *New York Times*, July 1, 1929, p. 52; Morris Gilbert, "Venezuela is Menaced by Shadow of Revolt," idem. August 25, 1929, p. 18; Leigh Stevenson, "Dictator Puts 25 Women in Crazy House," *Chicago Daily Tribune*, March 27, 1929, p. 27.

Autobiography now became Nogales preferred solution. Nogales had always written largely about what he had directly experienced. So when he had a long interview in San Juan, Puerto Rico in March of 1931 that was later published in the *New York Times*, he described a series of sketches of his life that he was finishing, while also working on the aforementioned and never-completed "historical novel with a Near East setting."[187]

Having had unusual experiences in lands few had ever seen and fewer understood during World War I in the Middle East, and again in the mid-1920's in revolutionary Nicaragua, a fifty-two year old Nogales proceeded to weave a narrative of his life before World War I that mixed the true, the untrue and the half-true. In these chapters of his life, Nogales piled collections of untruths and half-truths on a foundation of the genuine and the real. He was someone *The New York Times* enthused about as a "real D'Artagnan," a romantic hero of his age in 1930. Nogales sought to expand his popularity with his tales of youthful derring-do.[188]

The tales Nogales told involved the completion of the abortive book about his years in the western United States, which Nogales had planned in 1926 and 1927. As we have seen, Nogales had originally produced a synopsis for a ghostwriter to complete, in a simple and action-oriented fashion that could make the book saleable "for the [movie] screen." Going back to the materials he had, Nogales finished up sections on his experiences as a gold prospector and traveler in Alaska, a mining surveyor and speculator in Nevada, and a cowboy along the Rio Grande border with Mexico. He then book-ended these materials with tales of his earlier life in Venezuela and Asia, and added more chapters of his military experiences in the Ottoman

187 Harwood Hull, "Nogales Discards His Sword for Pen... Will Write of Experience," *New York Times*, March 31, 1931, p. 52.
188 "Real D'Artagnans Who Seek Peril Afar," *New York Times Magazine*, April 27, 1930, p. 18.

Empire. Nogales then published this chronicle as *Memoirs of a Soldier of Fortune* in 1931 (in London) and in 1932 (in New York).[189]

A Man Who Loved Exiles

The fact that Nogales' most commercially successful (and still in-print) book appeared first in London was important. Nogales' memoir of his years as an Ottoman officer had made him literary, military, and political friendships there. One of these friendships, with Scottish writer Robert Bontine Cunninghame Graham, flourished in ways that benefitted Nogales' career in important ways. Cunninghame Graham, briefly put, was one of those writers who seemed, to many of his contemporaries, to have been everywhere and done everything. He also appeared to know everybody who was anybody in London's literary, critical, and political scene. Though a nobleman, Cunninghame Graham had served in Parliament as one of the very first Labour Party MPs and had even been imprisoned for inciting to riot in the 1890's. He had also spent his youth as a gaucho in South America and became the first honorary leader of The Scottish National Party in his old age. Unknown today, he was someone whom contemporaries as varied as T. E. Lawrence, George Bernard Shaw, Joseph Conrad, and William Henry Hudson spoke about in terms of deep and abiding respect. The man simply exuded and embodied style, averred George Bernard Shaw, no mean social, political, or literary stylist himself.[190]

Cunninghame Graham was also a man who loved exiles, because he had been one. He savored isolated underdogs who operated at the intersection – or the ragged edges – of cultures; again because he himself had repeatedly and variously done so. His non-fiction works

189 Nogales to Constance Murray Skinner, November 21, 1927, Skinner Papers, New York Public Library Archives.
190 Cedric Watts and Laurence Davies, *Cunninghame Graham: A Critical Biography* (Cambridge, Cambridge University Press, 1979); Herbert Faulkner West, *Robert Bontine Cunninghame Graham: His Life and Works* (London, Cranley and Day, 1932); A. F. Tschiffely, *Don Roberto... R. B. Cunninghame Graham, 1852-1936* (London, Heinemann, 1937).

alone included volumes of Moroccan travel, Latin-American history, and early literary efforts to ponder the dangers of racism and religious extremism and conflict. Cunningham Graham was drawn to those who translated (or tried to) sometimes-conflicting ideas across cultural and linguistic barriers. From self-styled literary and social "outlaws" like expatriate American writer Frank Harris to Moroccan sheikhs to exiled Polish sailor and novelist Joseph Conrad (whose closest friend in life he became), Cunninghame Graham was a magnificent, flamboyant, ironical, romantic, and paradoxical figure, whose life combined not-a-few opposites, but in ways that entranced more often than they infuriated or confused.[191]

By 1931, Nogales and celebrity literary figure Cunninghame Graham were close enough that Nogales could ask for, and get, a long and gracious seven page preface to his *Memoirs* from Cunninghame Graham. This preface helped significantly with believability and sales.[192]

There were ironies aplenty in a well-known and widely respected author introducing Nogales to a British audience. Graham had spent time in the American West himself; been a gaucho in South America; and travelled the interior Llanos high plains of Venezuela across which Nogales had sometimes raided. Cunninghame Graham, in short, was not an easy man to lie to. He knew, accordingly, that some of what Nogales said about himself was inflated and embroidered. Savoring the irony, he titled the original handwritten draft of his Preface to Nogales' memoirs as the "Life and Miracles of General Rafael De Nogales."[193]

---

191 For Conrad, see: Cedric T. Watts, *Joseph Conrad's Letters to R. B. Cunninghame Graham* (Cambridge. Cambridge University Press, 1969). Conrad and Cunninghame Graham's friendship lasted from 1897 to Conrad's death in 1924. Frank Harris, *Contemporary Portraits: Third Series* (New York, published by the author, 1920), pp. 45-60.
192 Rafael De Nogales, *Memoirs of a Soldier of Fortune* (London, Wright and Brown [1931], esp. vii-xiii.

Gentle (and private) "Life and Miracles" mockery aside, Graham dropped this title and followed it up with very generous words that only-just preserved Nogales' legitimacy with both the reviewer for the *Times Literary Supplement* and at the hands of well-known critic V. S. Pritchett in the *Spectator*. The *Times* reviewer, for instance, said that portions of the book read like "the daydream of some elderly civilian in the Education Office" before a combination of

Robert Bontine Cunninghame Graham

Cunninghame Graham's prefatory sponsorship and enlightenment, and Nogales' "vivid disjointed style" reassured them. Pritchett remarked in the *Spectator*, meanwhile, that "It is the kind of book which moves one to murmur 'Liar' at passages which sound like pure Hollywood, but whose naïveté and consistency oblige one to take back the accusation."[194]

Moreover, at precisely the same time, Nogales' *The Looting of Nicaragua* was also republished in London. This was a handsome and well-illustrated revised edition, with the glowing introduction by an anti-imperialist Labour Party MP, who was also a supporter of

193 Cunninghame Graham's draft of his Preface to Nogales' book is in the National Library of Scotland Collections; Cunninghame Graham papers, Box 103, folder 2.
194 *Times Literary Supplement*, October 29, 1931, p. 833; *Spectator*, January 16, 1932, p. 87.

Mahatma Gandhi, as previously discussed. What Nogales later termed Graham's "many and delicate favors" – probably of a financial nature – helped make the simultaneous appearance of these two books possible.[195]

What caused Cunninghame Graham to assist the career of a middle-aged Venezuelan whom he knew was more than capable of telling tales truer than the truth?

Here, it helps to know that Cunninghame Graham knew both Nogales and T. E. Lawrence personally. He appreciated that both told tall stories, exaggerated their achievements, took liberties with truth and suppressed shortcomings. He was an unromantic romantic who thought the world's peoples were different but not necessarily better than each other. Like Nogales, he had started writing about exotic lands and locales at about the age of forty; and, again like him, he had often mined his personal experience in order to do it. He knew what the term "literary license" was – and he had used it in telling his travel tales. Again like Nogales, he had a temperament that former Prime Minister Ramsay MacDonald said was like that of a "soldier of fortune ... fighting towards some great ideal." Cunninghame Graham's ideals included Socialism. He had originally opposed British entry into World War I, and he also – as an admirer of Spanish culture and civilization, as well as a man whose first and only wife was Spanish – heartily disliked U.S. military expansion and control in the Caribbean and Central America. Cunninghame Graham had seen conservative imperialists like Winston Churchill laud T. E. Lawrence (with help from Dream Merchant Lowell Thomas) as a "supremely fine representative of the vigor, daring, imagination, humility and learning of youth", and seen that opinion enthusiastically picked-up

---

195 For Nogales' inflated claims that the Secretary of the Navy was behind the libel suit for $250,000.00 by the single Marine officer who had halted distribution of the original edition see, Rafael De Nogales, *The Looting of Nicaragua* (London, Wright and Brown [1931], p. 8.

Robert Bontine Cunninghame Graham

on the other side of the Atlantic as well, "in ways" one of Lawrence's recent biographers writes, "that now seem rather embarrassing."[196]

Cunninghame Graham the anti-imperialist, therefore, never believed the hype about Lawrence of Arabia in the first place. He had seen a lot of official lying and Anglo-Saxon imperialist triumphalism in his day. Born in 1852, he had a front row seat on the creation of a global British empire on which the sun never set. His ancestors and relatives had helped build, maintain, and protect that dominion. He knew that fictions about exotic lands masqueraded as facts. This knowledge amused more than it amazed. A proud Scot who co-founded the Scottish National Party and served as its first president, Cunninghame Graham also had a great and enduring interest in "loser" or "runner-up" cultures which his youth in South America

---

196 Tschiffley, op. cit, p. 440 (Ramsay MacDonald quote); William Chace, "T. E. Lawrence: The Uses of Heroism" in Jeffrey Meyers (ed), *T. E. Lawrence: Soldier, Writer, Legend: New Essays* (New York, St. Martin's, 1989), p. 129.

and his marriage to a daughter of a Spanish noble family did absolutely nothing to moderate. Just as Scotland had finally lost its independence to English kings after centuries of struggle, so Spain and its American empire stretching from the Rio Grande to Tierra del Fuego had lost imperial, political, technological, and economic races to the British and the (English-speaking) Americans. George Washington, accordingly, was remembered and revered, Cunninghame Graham wrote and believed, while Latins whose political and military genius was fully equivalent to his (like Simon Bolivar of Venezuela) had to make-do with footnotes – if that – in (English language) histories produced by the dominant culture.[197]

That Cunninghame Graham had an oft-remarked preference for those underdogs downtrodden by imperialism or capitalism did not mean that he, any more than Nogales, was enamored of Noble Savages or victims of evil conquerors, including the Ottoman Turks. Such romanticism they left to others – including the young T. E. Lawrence. Instead, to Cunninghame Graham and Nogales, man was a "violent exploitative animal." Unfortunates, as one of Graham's biographers summarized, could be "more sinned against, but they [did] their share of sinning too." What resulted was a hierarchy of exploitation: in which stronger groups oppressed weaker; weaker groups abused still weaker ones; and those most oppressed at the bottom of the power pyramid terrorized whom they could. Kurds, Arabs, and Armenians were not very ethically noble to Rafael De Nogales. The Turks were simply better armed and organized and acted as ruthlessly as their opponents would have done – but before they did.[198]

This fundamental concept that men suffered, but were not, accordingly, noble, was not quite in the romantic mainstream. Nor

---

197 See, i.e., F. B. Cunninghame Graham, *The Conquest of New Granada,* reprint of 1926 edition, (New York, Kraus Reprint ed., 1967), p. 7, ftn.
198 Watts and Davies, op. cit., p. Tschiffely, op cit., p. 101; Cedric Watts, R. B. Cunninghame Graham (Boston, Twayne Publishers, 1983), p. 33.

was it bathed in adolescent or scholarly volumes of Arthurian legend or medieval chivalry. Men like Cunninghame Graham and Joseph Conrad and Rafael De Nogales had done a lot of living before they ever began to put pen to paper. Their knight errantry – literary or otherwise – could be courageous and gallant; but it did not assume that the deity which watched over it and them was anything but indifferent and even callous a large majority of the time. God was also not British (or American), and there was no guarantee whatsoever that everything would turn out all right. Half romantic and half cynic, Cunninghame Graham could write to a friend who later edited the first edition of T. E. Lawrence's letters that life was "... a joke, a black joke ... but we must laugh at our own efforts." Thirty-five years later, Field Marshal Edmund Allenby, in an introduction to Nogales' last book (one dedicated to Cunninghame Graham) explained that "Rafael De Nogales tells us that 'Life is a joke and occasionally a very bad joke.'"[199]

Both Cunninghame Graham and Nogales, therefore, could be self-dramatizing celebrities; but self-important individuals they generally were not. Caring about losers, for example, alerted them to the virtues of tolerance and the dangers of arrogance. Nogales had destroyed Armenians, Russians, Kurds, Arabs, Australians and Britons for the Ottoman military; and then watched while a 500 year old Turkish empire ceased to exist in its turn. Cunninghame Graham had been part of bloody gaucho rebellions, whose victorious leaders were later destroyed by national armies. Because both were aware of the sometimes sudden twists of fate, both tended to argue for more understanding and respect for other peoples who would, one day, come to have their place in the sun. They argued for cultural modesty as intelligently selfish self-interest. Though neither man was free of prejudice (Cunninghame Graham, i.e., had the fashionable anti-

---

199 Watts and Davies, op. cit., p. 171, 197; Edmund Allenby, introduction to Rafael De Nogales, *Silk Hat and Spurs* (London, Wright and Brown, [1934]. pp. v, viii, 236.

Semitism of British aristocracy; while Nogales tended to view Arabs as a lot of "rabble" which could only be treated with the fist and the sword), both were among a very small minority of writers to whom most of the standard bigotries of the era in which they lived did not apply.[200]

Added to all these general conceptual similarities were three more likenesses of an immediate kind. Nogales and Cunninghame Graham were both excellent horsemen and horse lovers; Cunninghame Graham knew and loved Venezuela as Nogales did; and, finally, Cunninghame Graham despised Venezuela's Juan Vicente Gomez with as cold a ferocity as Nogales himself. Referring both to the dictator's fecundity in fathering children out of wedlock and his ferocity in torturing and killing political enemies, Cunninghame Graham quipped that Gomez "had no morals either in the giving or the taking of life." On long visits to Venezuela and Colombia in 1925-1926 and 1926-1927, the Scots author also pointedly refused official invitations to meet Gomez in the presidential palace. Venezuelans died for far less.[201]

In the years between the first appearance of his *Memoirs of a Soldier of Fortune* in London in 1931 and July of 1933, Nogales had good reason to thank his "valued and astute friend" Cunninghame Graham for "many and delicate favors." What those exact favors were will likely remain unknown; but they certainly involved literary advice and introductions. Publication in London – with likely financial help

---

200   For a flash of Graham's anti-Semitism, see: Tschiffely, pp. 380-81; also see Nogales, *Silk Hat and Spurs*, pp. 237, 238. For Arab "rabble" (and the statement that "we Turks knew how to handle" them. Plus a comment on an "insolent Sudanese darkey" who disobeyed an order Nogales gave to him, when both were in the Turkish army. Nogales' "we Turks" statement speaks quiet volumes regarding the point being made here.
201   Tschiffely, op. cit., p. 388; among Graham's writings preceding his mid-20s trips are: *Cartagena and the Banks of the Sinu* (New York, Doran and London, Heinemann, 1921). See also "The Plains of Venezuela" in A. F. Tschiffely (ed.), *Rodeo: A Collection of the Tales and Sketches of R. B. Cunninghame Graham* (New York, Literary Guild, 1938), pp. 46-53.

from Graham – also assisted publication of Nogales' *Memoirs* in New York the following year.[202]

"Soldier of Fortune"

Memoirs of a Soldier of Fortune was reviewed much less skeptically in the United States than it was in London. The *New York Times*, a longtime advocate and supporter, carried a long positive review. Nogales' talent for expanding his experience and importance was only obliquely referred to. All of his adventures "must be true in the larger fact, and most ... are probably accurate in detail," concluded the *Times*. The *New Republic*, which had liked his book on Nicaragua, liked *Memoirs* too. Again, an oblique reference was made to exaggeration and even fantasy; but in conclusion the magazine's reviewer said Nogales wrote "of his own savage and voluptuous country ... intimately, lovingly and with complete familiarity." The *Saturday Review of Literature*, meanwhile, had hated *The Looting of Nicaragua*, but, in a much longer review of *Memoirs*, lauded "A D'Artagnan of Today." Yet again, the reviewer noted exaggeration in *Memoirs of a Soldier of Fortune*, but concluded, overall, that "one gets a general impression of candor, essential truth, and a likeable clear-headedness and common sense." Far away in Australia, where Nogales' Nicaragua book had received good reviews, his *Memoirs*, helped along by press interviews with one of his former captives who was then a Cabinet minister, got good reviews in the Melbourne

---

202 A clear point arguing for Graham's monetary support is that publishers almost-never put two books by single authors they have never published before in-print in a single year. This Wright and Brown did with Nogales' *Memoirs*, and the new edition of his Nicaragua book. Rafael De Nogales to Cunninghame Graham (in Spanish), July 19, 1933, correspondence files, Cunninghame Graham Papers, National Archives of Scotland; Rafael De Nogales, *Memoirs of a Soldier of Fortune* (New York, Harrison Smith, 1932 and New York, Garden City Publishing, 1932). (The only difference between these two editions is that several photos appearing in the former are deleted in the latter. Garden City publishing appears to have purchased Harrison Smith publishing and done new printing(s) of the book.

papers. Of all Nogales' works, his advertisement of himself as a Soldier of Fortune won him by-far his largest readership, both in his own lifetime and since.[203]

In *Memoirs*, however, Nogales also clearly started crossing lines between exaggeration and lying. We have earlier seen, for example, that Nogales tended to exaggerate his own self-importance. If additionally, for example, as many Young Turk notables and "political" military commanders had wanted him dead as he occasionally claimed, he would not have survived his first year as a "yuzbashi", or captain, in the cavalry of the Ottoman Army.

Nogales the literary man, however, was nothing if not public about what he was doing. To differentiate truth from fiction, then, let us begin with the very first claim that Nogales made about his life of action. "At the outbreak of the Spanish-American War," he told the *New York Times* in 1931, "he answered his first urge for battle by joining the Spaniards. Commissioned a second lieutenant, he was wounded at [the battle of] Santiago and returned to Spain." Though referenced only in-passing in Cunninghame Graham's introduction to *Memoirs*, Nogales expanded this claim into a brief chapter in the sequel volume to *Memoirs*, titled *Silk Hat and Spurs*.[204]

In all probability, this whole story is false. There are four things that combat veterans usually remember about wartime experiences

---

203   Percy Hutchison, "Adventure all over the Map," *New York Times*, February 21, 1932, p. 12; David Minot Young, "Any Old War Will Do," *The New Republic*, Vol. 70 (April 27, 1932), pp. 306-07; "A D'Artagnan of Today," *Saturday Review of Literature*, Vol. 8 (February 13, 1932), pp. 519-20 (contrast with the same magazine's review of *The Looting of Nicaragua* in Vol. 4 (March 31, 1928), pp. 725-26); Trouble is Enough," *Time*, February 29, 1932; "Soldier of Fortune: Adventures of Gen. Nogales," *Melbourne Herald*, January 13, 1934, p. 37. (For favorable treatment of the Nicaragua book, see clipping headed "M.P." May 20, 1932 and titled "An Object Lesson in Dollar Diplomacy". Both these latter clippings are courtesy of Colonel T. H. White's daughter, Ms. Judith Harley, and also come courtesy of the rare intellectual generosity of Dr. Brian Wimborne of Isaacs, Australian Capital Territory.

with especial clarity: their units, their commanders, their comrades-in-arms, and the battles they survived. Nogales' stories of his military service mention only the best-known (in the U.S.A.) land battle of the Spanish-American War. No military unit, commanders, or comrades' names are mentioned. All this vagueness makes it difficult, at best, to find Nogales' service record, or to determine what (unmentioned) medal he supposedly won. Spanish diplomats in the Ottoman Empire apparently had the same trouble during World War I, when, as Turkish historian Mehmet Necati Kutlu discovered, Nogales made a request for his Spanish-American war medal from Jerusalem on October 4, 1916.[205]

Further difficulties exist on the civilian side of Nogales' story. Nogales' most recent and thorough Venezuelan biographer, Mirela Quero De Trinca, notes that both the Spanish Duchess who supposedly got Nogales to volunteer and the Captain-General of Nueva Leon she was supposedly married to in his story were both "fantasy figures." Further, Nogales' Spanish-American war service accounts as recorded in the *New York Times*, in the introduction to *Memoirs*, and in the sequel to *Memoirs* that closely followed differ, in important respects, from the version he wrote in an essay for a U.S.-based adventure magazine in the early 1930s. Finally, though several Venezuelan investigators of Nogales' career have discovered that "a Venezuelan general, Leonardo Corcuera, put himself at the disposal of the Spanish cause" in the Spanish-American War, it is very unlikely that Nogales, aged only eighteen in 1898, would ever have been mistaken for such a senior military man.[206]

---

204 Harwood Hull, "Nogales Discards His Sword for Pen..." *New York Times*, March 31, 1931, p. 52; Cunninghame Graham told the tale for Nogales in his introduction to *Memoirs* (p. xi); Nogales told his tale himself in his *Silk Hat and Spurs* (London, Wright and Brown [1934], pp. 12-15.
205 Nogales' request is produced in facsimile in Kutlu, *Turkiye'de Bir Gezgin Sovalye Nogales Mendez* (Istanbul, Gendas, 2000), p. 125.
206 De Trinca, pp. 105-07.

Fabrication and Falsehood

What led Nogales to fabricate and falsify? De Trinca argues persuasively that Nogales fell prey to his own celebrity. He did this by providing ever-more-dramatic tales of romantic action to attract readers and regard. In the process, a real-life adventurer who had maintained a toehold in world history for twenty years crossed over the line from exaggeration into fantasy.[207]

Taking this path was as tragic as it was unnecessary. The truths of Nogales' life hardly lacked for excitement. His first book gave him a modest version of the same sort of repute in the United States and England that T. E. Lawrence enjoyed. He was a gentleman-warrior fighting in little-known lands full of Biblical renown. Nogales' tales, however, were ones of survival, not triumph. He also did not automatically presume the superiority of English imperialism over Ottoman imperialism, or the preeminence of Christian groups over Muslim groups in the culture quilt that was the Middle East. While Lawrence treated his Turkish opponents as either brutal or inept, Nogales defended the honor of the Ottoman Army and the courage of the vast majority of his ethnic Turkish comrades-in-arms. This approach was decidedly unusual in an era when Greek, Armenian, U.S. Protestant missionary, or Australian commentators often had no difficulty whatever arguing that the cruelties of the "Unspeakable Turk" demonstrated the essential barbarism of an entire society.[208]

Nogales' narrative in *Four Years Beneath the Crescent* was also unusual in that the vast majority of German officers cooperating with

207 ibid.
208 Two examples from T. E. Lawrence's *Seven Pillars of Wisdom* are chapters CXVII in a section entitled "The Turk Manner" (massacre of children and raping and killing of women possibly by the Turkish cavalry unit with which Nogales had served) and Chapter LXXX (torture and rape by the Turkish garrison of Deraa in Syria that caused Lawrence to write that "the citadel of my integrity had been irrevocably lost." Thomas H. White's *Guests of the Unspeakable* is full of charges that Turkish captors consciously starved Britsh, Indian and Australian prisoners who were not officers to death.

the Ottoman military effort simply ignored inconvenient events like the Armenian massacres. Nogales' best and often-conflicted tales of his wartime experience, meanwhile, provided support for all four of the major explanations of the events that began in Eastern Anatolia in 1915. These were, first, that what happened was a centralized policy of ethnic cleansing and massacre largely controlled by Interior Minister Talaat Bey. A second explanation, civil war, argued that massacres followed localized Armenian rebellions, conspiracies, and mass desertions pre-dating the start of large scale killings. The third explanation put the responsibility for massacres on especially murderous district governors or local officials who hired bandits to kill refugees en route, without centralized orders or encouragement from Constantinople. The fourth and final explanation blamed supply, transportation and sanitary problems that produced widespread mortality within an Empire which, by 1917, was very hard-pressed even to feed, clothe, or provide basic medical assistance to its soldiers in Syria, Palestine, and Mesopotamia.[209]

Nogales' first book, a poetic, sometimes wrenching and at other times callous tale of wartime survival in a doomed empire, was followed by his passionate attack on the formal and informal empire that the United States was creating in Central America and the Caribbean. This flawed but nevertheless pioneering effort received respectful attention and significant reviews on both sides of the

209 For the toxic mix of racism and Social Darwinism that caused few German officers to notice or report massacres, see: Isabel V. Hull, *Absolute Destruction: Military Culture and Practices of War in Imperial Germany* (Ithaca, Cornell University Presses, 2004), pp. 263-90 and Hilmar Kaiser (in collaboration with Luther and Nancy Eskijian, *At the Crossroads of der Zor: Death, Survival, and Humanitarian Resistance in Aleppo, 1915-1917* (Princeton, New Jersey and London, Gomidas Institute, 2002). German consul Walter Rossler, Aleppo Governor Djelal Bey (until his replacement in June, 1915) and various Ottoman officials, police officers, and Muslim civilians (especially women) number among the heroes in Kaiser's narrative about Pastor Hovhannes Eskijian. See pp. 14-15, 16, 40-41, 42, 49-50, 60, and 71.

Atlantic. Again, Nogales was speaking about – and for – peoples regarding whom most educated Americans were culturally, linguistically, and historically ignorant. Nogales also read the future of revolution in Nicaragua better than the man who soon became U.S. Secretary of State. He understood the importance of rebel leaders like August Sandino so well that Carleton Beals, the reporter who built his own literary reputation by introducing Sandino to U.S. readers in the *Nation* magazine the year after *Looting of Nicaragua* was – briefly – published, later called Nogales' understanding of events and personalities "remarkable."[210]

Remembering Armenians

In March, 1931, a 51½ year old Rafael De Nogales was in San Juan, Puerto Rico; probably mostly engaged in visiting his friends Luis Munoz Marin and Muna Lee. During the trip, he gave a lengthy interview to an independent journalist whose work was later published in the *New York Times*. This interview included a tale that Nogales had never told in-print before, and which spoke volumes about his inability to bury his early wartime experiences in Eastern Anatolia early in 1915.

Nogales' tale concerned "an almost perfect friendship, a year's intimate companionship that was without a flaw." The intimacy involved Nogales and an Armenian boy named Azerdjan. He "went everywhere" with Nogales, "never talked back, never contradicted, never betrayed a confidence." Azerdjan also "never intruded when or where not wanted, and was loyal to the last." This perfection of friendship and intimacy only had one major flaw. Azerdjan was, in fact, the human skull of a young Armenian boy of about 16 who had died in one of the first villages that Nogales visited on the road to

---

210 "New Nicaraguan Revolt Predicted by Nogales," *New York Times*, July 11, 1927, p. 12; Carleton Beals, *Banana Gold* (Philadelphia, Lippincott, 1932); Carleton Beals, *Glass Houses: Ten Years of Free-Lancing* (Philadelphia, Lippincott, 1938), p. 254. Beals, ironically, mis-remembered the title of Nogales' book as *The Rape of Nicaragua*.

Van. Azerdjan, as Nogales later reconstructed the tale, was apparently one of the seven Armenian males that Nogales had tried, and failed, to protect in Adil Javus on April 21, 1915, as his introduction to the dynamics of hell in very small places began. In the new version of the tale, Azerdjan was the last male survivor in his village. He threw himself at Ottoman officer Nogales' feet and asked for his protection. Nogales then talked with the boy and said: "Azerdjan, you and I are the only Christians in many miles. Soon I alone will be left. You have no chance. I can do nothing. In the name of the Christ whose faith you profess, die like a Christian, like a man. Show these dogs you are not afraid."[211]

Azerdjan then, in Nogales' tale, "straightened himself and walked to his death, emitting as classic curses against the Turks as Nogales had ever heard in any tongue." Given that Nogales had only been in the Ottoman Empire since January of 1915, was not, on his own testimony, fluent in Turkish, and could not understand Armenian, this ferociously ironic tale was also a literary invention: one which he later used and further elaborated on in his final book of memoirs, published in London in 1934.[212]

Literary inventions like this, however, allowed Nogales to engage in a kind of imaginary dialogue with a brave Armenian male: one who had died in the right (i.e. Latin American) way: unafraid and like a true warrior; unconquered to the last.

This dialogue, in turn, was accomplished by another set of elaborations on fact. During one of Nogales' (probably actual) inspection tours as "Acting-Inspector of the Cavalry of the 11 Caucasus Army" in 1917, Nogales found himself with little to do in Diarbekir, site of some of the largest early mass killings of Armenian males. He then saw some soldiers digging a trench he suddenly claimed to recognize as the very site where the brave young Armenian

211 Harwood Hull, "Nogales Discards his Sword for a Pen...Will Write of Experience...", *New York Times*, March 31, 1931, p. 53.
212 Rafael De Nogales, *Silk Hat and Spurs*, pp. 52-53.

had been killed two years before. Further recognizing Azerdjan by the gunshot to his head which had killed him, Nogales recovered the skull and told his Albanian orderly Tasim Chavush to "take it home with him while I looked around for a suitable place to bury it."

For the next six months to a year (his accounts differ) Nogales then had an alter ego. "We talked well into the night," was all he told the *New York Times*. In his final book, *Silk Hat and Spurs*, he was slightly more forthcoming. Nogales in this expanded version spent many nights alone reading. During one of these "literary orgies," he seemed to be greeted in friendship by Azerdjan's skull, which was then lying atop a pile of books. Responding in kind he and the skull "became buddies at once."

"From that time on," Nogales continued, "every night, after I had done my reading, we used to start a pleasant conversation in German and made a clean breast of it all by confiding to each other our little troubles without anybody being the wiser, because my orderly did not understand a word of German."[213]

From intimate friend, the remains of the brave young Armenian swiftly advanced to the ranks of father confessor. Nogales told him all his frustrations and fears, in the certainty of utter and complete confidence. The dead would keep the secrets about the dead; while Nogales, meanwhile, had his brave and courageous young Armenian for friendship.

In return for all of this admission, purging, and disclosure, Nogales eventually took the skull back to Constantinople with him and insured that his silent Armenian friend received a Christian burial, probably with Catholic monks.[214]

What, precisely, Nogales admitted to – major, minor, or in-between – is unknown. Like many a combat veteran before and since, Nogales may have felt that experienced warriors already understood what he had told his Armenian alter ego/father confessor, while the

213 ibid., p. 54.
214 ibid.

inexperienced simply lacked the experiential equipment to even begin
to comprehend what was involved.

Nogales' lengthy monologues – however actual or metaphorical –
testify to the continuing effect of the events of early 1915 on Nogales'
mind. By the early 1930s, the events in and around Anatolia in 1915-
1916 were receding fast from political and cultural awareness. U.S.
Protestant denominations had invested tens of millions of dollars –
huge sums for the time – in caring for survivors and orphans in the
United States and the Middle East. Armenian-Americans, generally,
however, lacked strong domestic U.S. political allies. Most
Armenians were not Protestant or Catholic converts. For that
minority which was, Protestant churches avoided political agitation
to protect their remaining congregations and religious institutions in
Turkey. A bloody Greek invasion of Turkey from 1920 to 1922
muddied already muddy ethical waters and did nothing to cast
Christian societies as groups only interested in peaceful coexistence
with Muslim nations. The same head of the U.S. Department of State
who had determined that Venezuela's dictator Juan Vicente Gomez
was a necessary – and profitable – evil also determined that the "well-
known disloyalty" of the Armenians and the "fact that territory they
inhabited was within the zone of military operations" had clearly
justified wartime removals. U.S. ambassador Henry Morgenthau and
U.S. consular officials had both protested horrible brutalities. But this
had not led the U.S. either to declare war on the Ottoman Empire
during the war or to seek to exercise any policing power in the Middle
East after the war. Efforts to have a postwar U.S. protectorate over
Armenia, for example, died as still-born as T. E. Lawrence's hopes for
an independent Arab government in Syria. The Wilsonian doctrine
of the rights to national self-determination of peoples was not a
matter for any but "Europeans" (a definition which then often
excluded "Orientals" including Armenians, Japanese, Iranians and
Arabs, as well as Turks, Latin Americans and Jews.)[215]

215   Daniel, op cit, p. 256; Krenn, op. cit., p. 102.

Between 1927 and 1934, therefore, full diplomatic and trade recognition – broken off in 1917 – was restored between the United States and the new secular Turkish Republic established by Mustafa Kemal (Ataturk). Armenian-Americans campaigned long and hard against Congressional ratification of agreements. But they were hampered by sometimes-bloody splits within the Armenian Apostolic Church in America and among Armenians debating whether or not to support a Bolshevik-created Union of Soviet Socialist Republics which had within it a (nominally) independent Armenian Soviet Socialist Republic: the closest thing remaining to an Armenian national homeland.[216]

General American interest in matters-Armenian, never widespread, only decreased further. Like Turkey, Nicaragua and Venezuela, Armenia was one of those little miscellaneous places which few Americans knew about, and far fewer had visited. It was full of sound and fury that was hard for most high school or college-educated Americans to signify anything about. Even these minorities (or small minorities) of the adult population had little awareness of any of the prominent economic, strategic, or political points at issue. It was all so much "white noise" to them. They lacked the basic analytic "hooks" on which to hang basic ideas that could span the gulfs between ethnic grudges and rationalizations. If you ask most educated and aware Americans today why between 300,000 and 1 million people died in 1965 in Indonesia in an political, ethnic, and religious struggle that almost tore the country apart, and which the U.S. Central Intelligence Agency termed "one of the worst mass murders of the 20th century," few but the occasional journalist or Peace Corps volunteer or international businessman will have any idea what you are talking about. Perhaps a few Americans will recall a then-unknown American-Australian actor named Mel Gibson and a young actress named Sigourney Weaver in a rarely-seen and foreign-

---

216 Merrill D. Peterson, op cit., pp. 153 ff provides a brief summary of these events and disputes.

directed film, "The Year of Living Dangerously." That, however, will be that. So it very largely was with events in an Ottoman Empire whose cultures and peoples still too-largely remain terra incognita.

It was as well, then, that Nogales spoke with his skull, in his Hamlet-like monologue. There were few others for the aging Venezuelan to talk to about his experiences. Even fewer of those who did know anything would have had any interest in talking with him about the unedited versions of the grim (or other) realities he had experienced.

Chapter Eight

Megalomania and Myth Making

Had Rafael De Nogales stopped with his second book, he would now occupy a secure and modest place in history as a commentator whose unusual degrees of linguistic facility and intercultural adaptability allowed him to bridge European and non-European worlds and examine the "entangled histories" of Western and non-Western peoples – all of this taking place in an era where the degrees of racial and religious egalitarianism Nogales expressed were very rare indeed at any level of American (or other) society.

Nogales, however, wanted to be more than an intercultural interpreter. He also wanted fame, the kind of fame that T. E. Lawrence had. Adding legends, grand adventures, and romance to his early life would, he hoped, keep editors and readers interested and insure his career as an independent journalist would stay vigorous and profitable in unsettled economic times. Nogales' many travels, after all, did not come cheap. Meeting and charming people at their clubs in London required that Nogales had to – in his own words – "live up to style." Tensions and disagreements with distributors of Nogales' works in areas like Central America were regular and severe. As well, costs of writing in a language not his own included paying his literary agent to finish-up and polish his prose.[217]

It was not surprising; therefore, that among the people Nogales cultivated was a popular U.S. print, radio and movie journalist. Myth-maker and Dream Merchant Lowell Thomas had done more

---

217 Nogales to Skinner, May 30, 1928, p. 4 (second side of sheet); Nogales to Skinner, March 30, 1927; Nogales to S. W. Sanders of D. Appleton & Company, December 28, 1929 – all in Skinner Papers, New York Public Library Archives.

than any other single person on Earth to turn T. E. Lawrence into a celebrity of the English-speaking world. What Thomas had done for "Lawrence of Arabia", Nogales hoped Thomas could help him accomplish as well. This could be achieved by both advertising *Memoirs of a Soldier of Fortune* and by getting the sequel to *Memoirs* published in the United States.[218]

Thomas may well have used his considerable connections to assist Nogales in finding an American publisher for *Memoirs* in the depths of the Great Depression. Otherwise he did relatively little for Nogales. His introduction to the U.S. edition of *Memoirs* had grandiose but catchy lines like "To call Rafael de Nogales picturesque would be banal. He comes nearest to being the true soldier of fortune of any man I know." Most of the two page summary of Nogales' career that followed, however, was a word-for-word repetition of what someone – almost surely Nogales himself – had written for the earlier London edition of the book. Thomas' advertisement then closed with another line of his own that:

> ... if Rafael de Nogales fails to become dictator of some hot country, he will probably end his wild career with a cigarette between his lips at sunrise.

Such puffery surely assisted sales. Lowell Thomas, after all, was nothing if not a popular entertainer and publicist who understood his times. Thomas, however, also apparently did absolutely nothing to help Nogales publish a follow-up volume of additional memoirs or to market them in Hollywood.[219]

Thomas' decisions to limit his involvement preserved his own repute. *Memoirs of a Soldier of Fortune* was a collection of genuine experiences enlivened by fantasies and exaggerations. The sequel, *Silk*

218 Nogales to Dr. Alex Hamilton Rice, November 21, 1931 (enclosed with a copy of the London edition of *Memoirs*), Inscriptions and Letters to Alex Hamilton Rice, New York Public Library Archives.
219 Lowell Thomas, introduction to the U.S. edition of *Memoirs of a Soldier of Fortune* (New York, Harrison Smith, 1932), pp. vii-viii.

Hat and Spurs, published in London in 1934, was a series of potboiler magazine stories badly strung-together and featuring utter falsehoods (including Nogales participating in a rebel raid on the Venezuelan coast that looked a lot too much like the "Falke" raid of 1929 that Nogales had earlier and ostentatiously criticized.) *Memoirs* of 1931 and 1932 featured a base of real experiences in Alaska, Nevada, along the Mexican border, and in Turkey and Venezuela. *Silk Hat and Spurs* of 1934 featured Nogales gaily prancing around the world between 1898 and 1900 intensively visiting 13 countries and colonies in North Africa, Asia, South Africa, South America, and the Caribbean; fighting in a war and two rebellions; and in-between all this shooting elephants (or leopards) and meeting fascinating or simply fantastic characters. There is no doubt Nogales did some of these things. The likelihood of him doing most or all of them to the extents he claimed to have done them is zero.[220]

What was the megalomania all about? Why, in addition to visiting places, did Nogales make a series of impossible claims that he had enrolled in armies from the Moroccan to the Japanese, to fight enemies as various as frontier tribes and the armies of the Czar of all the Russians?

Nogales was, as part of the answer, increasingly achieving in fiction what he could not accomplish in fact. His career as a rebel was one of continuing, grinding, frustrating, failure. By early 1931, for instance, Nogales was bravely and rightfully denouncing Juan Vicente Gomez's son, a thorough scoundrel, for corruption in granting oil concessions. He then sought yet again to overthrow dictator "El Benemerito" himself. This time he formed a revolutionary committee in London with fellow exile Humberto Blanco Fombona and others. But, once again, Gomez's spy service proved adept at impeding "a conference that he tried to give about the situation in Venezuela at the 'Anglo-Spanish Society,' as well as the publication of an article in a daily of this city." Following Nogales'

220 *Silk Hat and Spurs*, pp 57-72, 101, 128.

steps with the "greatest discretion" because of Nogales' "several important relationships" with men like Cunninghame Graham and Field Marshall Allenby, the Venezuelan embassy's resident spymaster, ambassador Diogenes Escalante, saw Nogales as, at one and the same time, a buffoon, a charlatan, a dangerous terrorist, and a Bolshevik, and, so, acted accordingly to undermine any and all efforts Nogales made.[221]

After a decade and a half of persecution by well-funded political creatures like Escalante, Nogales was getting tired. His independence and – especially – his lack of commitment to institutions and organizations meant there was no network of support for him to rely upon when times were bad. Nogales operated as he almost-always had – as a loner, and one who was only at the periphery of most Venezuelan rebel networks, particularly those created by the "Generation of 1928."[222]

Just as Nogales was increasingly peripheral to Venezuelan exile politics, he seemed to stay distant and peripheral to his own family. In none of his writings in English is any member of his family ever mentioned in any capacity. Venezuelan diplomatic and spy service records note several visits Nogales made in Europe to a sister married to a German nobleman in the 1920's. The only specifically family issue Nogales handled as the oldest and only son was traveling to Curacao in 1928 to determine whether a man resident in Peru for 40 years was also a recognized illegitimate son of his father. (He wasn't.) Given that both Nogales' parents had died in his youth, memories of parents he had never – or, in the case of his mother, rarely – seen after the age of seven might have been precious. Nogales, however, wove nothing about either his family or his part-Indian background into any of the narratives he devised. *Recogido* illegitimacy later hesitantly accepted within a family without male children could help explain

221 De Trinca, p. 84.
222 I take this idea from: John A. Briton, *Carleton Beals: A Radical Journalist in Latin America* (University of New Mexico Press, 1987), p. 4.

why Nogales sought to inflate his own daredevil experiences, while obscuring his personal background.[223]

Given that Nogales so often used his own life as material, it is relevant he also discussed, at one point in his *Memoirs*, why he "enjoyed the curious alternations" of his life.

"There is something in human nature that enjoys a double life. Probably ... a dissatisfaction with the one life that has been allotted to us in the great counting-house of Fate, or a chafing feeling of being imprisoned in the same hide and the same personality for too long a time."[224]

Twice in his life, Nogales also elaborated in *Memoirs*, he had "taken a great resolution" to change his behavior and to "become a soldier and a scholar – at no matter what price." The first was at age sixteen and a half in 1895-1896, "after six disgraceful months ... in Paris in silk hat and formal dress." The second was circa 1901-1902, after what Nogales now claimed was his first attempt to invade Venezuela to overthrow the government. In both cases, Nogales wanted to "quit being a gilded youth" and "to quit walking on dead man's legs", by abandoning luxury and "earning my living with a sword, soldier of fortune style."[225]

In reality, Nogales seems to have earned his living prospecting, surveying, riding, selling mining claims, and writing for most of the years preceding World War I, with only occasional periods of rebellion thrown in (in 1911 and 1913). Other later claims about soldiering seem, to this biographer, unlikely and invented. The Spanish-American war we have already discussed. Nogales also later variously said he had served in the Japanese army and received a medal or been a Japanese or Chinese spy. All these claims (made in writings and interviews from 1931 to 1934) are also probably false. Then Nogales claimed to have fought for Ricardo Flores Magon, an

---

223 De Trinca, pp. 81-82.
224 Nogales, *Memoirs*, p. 128.
225 Nogales, *Memoirs*, pp. 21-25.

intellectual precursor of the Mexican Revolution of 1910-1920, in raids into northern Mexico circa 1908 and 1909. Though Nogales may have met Magon, who had taken refuge in the United States, it is not true, as Nogales claimed, that Magon himself led rebel armies in northern Mexico – or that Magon appointed Nogales as one of his regional lieutenants.[226]

When Nogales spun yarns about being a lieutenant of anarchist Flores Magon and providing early assistance to Magon's considerably more successful opponent Francisco Madero in *Memoirs*, written in 1931-1932, both key Mexican revolutionary leaders had been dead for ten years. Few were alive (and fewer of those spoke English) who could dispute Nogales' claims.

A Segmented News Environment

So it was with much of the past Nogales created for himself in his fifties, after his years of active campaigning had come to an end. As a multilingual man operating in many countries, he enjoyed what were then the benefits of a segmented news environment. Claims in one language did not have to be defended in another, because few of even the tiny minority of the college and university-educated in any nation were multi-lingual. Claims published in one country, similarly, did not have to be defended in another because of the costs of travel across oceans, and because of the lack of anything even remotely resembling today's instantaneous global electronic network in communication.

Examples are plentiful. Lawrence of Arabia did not begin to have some of his claims publicly deflated and debunked for twenty years after his death. He went out in a haze of glory when he died in 1935. The most egregious lies that were told about him – and from which he silently benefitted – were told by others, including journalist-entertainers like Lowell Thomas. Nogales, on the other hand, told his own lies about himself; in a language – and a culture – not his own.

226 Nogales, *Memoirs*, pp, 117, 118, 133 for inaccurate claims. (The previously cited books by Blaisdell, Albro, Raat, and MacLachlan all provide specifics on Flores Magon's career).

In the process, he far more promptly debunked himself. He died largely unknown and un-honored.

The editions of *Memoirs of a Soldier of Fortune* published in London and New York in 1931 and 1932 are instructive. Small specific lies can illustrate wider trends. Both editions, for example, close their narrative with Nogales meeting a young United States lieutenant after completing a long and exhausting expedition through the Nicaraguan jungles. Both editions have the young American officer recognizing Nogales' name and exclaiming that he had read Nogales' book *Four Years Beneath the Crescent* in the library at the U.S. Naval Academy in Annapolis.[227]

This story was identical to one Nogales first told in his *Looting of Nicaragua* book in 1928. Reality, however, was less dramatic. Nogales actually met the American officer when he first landed in Nicaragua, and before he had even set foot in a jungle. Nogales' fame also had not preceded him. The only reason the officer read Nogales' memoir of his four years as an Ottoman officer was that Nogales loaned his personal travel copy to him. So wrote Nogales to his friend and agent Constance Skinner from Puerto Cabezas, Nicaragua in March of 1927. Instead of a well-known explorer manfully struggling out of the jungle, an itinerant journalist and author had a pleasant conversation and dinner with a naval officer commanding a small port in eastern Nicaragua.[228]

Changes between editions and volumes also illustrated how Nogales could expand his own narrative importance. In the original U.S. edition of *The Looting of Nicaragua*, Nogales tells a personal tale of ferrying an important load of 200 pounds of salt to Liberal military leaders then fighting the Conservative armies allied with the United States. In a country undergoing civil war and loaded with bandits and

227 Nogales, *Memoirs*, p. 380 (USA ed.), p. 329 (UK ed.).
228 Nogales, *The Looting of Nicaragua* (New York, McBride, 1928), p. 227. Nogales to Skinner, March 30, 1927 (from Puerto Cabezas, Nicaragua), Skinner Papers, New York Public Library Archives.

deserters, trade was interrupted and scarcities of an essential preserving agent were widespread. So much so, Nogales recalled, that he was often ambushed by men who wanted his canoes, his guns, his ammunition, and, above all, his salt shipment. Finally, to help avoid further skirmishes, Nogales sent two of his men off to bury all the salt at a location unknown to him.[229]

In the London edition of the same book three years later, this whole section of a chapter and part of a following chapter were left out. The same story soon resurfaced, however, in the London edition of *Memoirs of a Soldier of Fortune*. Now, however, a livelier tale of avoiding military patrols was climaxed by Nogales and his canoeing companions being "suddenly and overwhelmingly surprised by the descent of a roaring wall of water which, I should judge, was fourteen feet high". Caused by a distant cloudburst in the mountains, this great flood almost killed Nogales and swept away most of his supplies, including the salt.[230]

From smaller exaggerations primarily aimed at feeding his literary and masculine ego, Nogales was now changing the basic narrative of his life to record heroic experiences he had never had. Things only got worse, as Nogales variously made or unmade grandiose claims about his youth and demonstrated a talent for self-promotion that fellow Venezuelan exiles could find irksome or worse.

The initial London edition of Nogales' *Memoirs*, for example, began with seven pages of staccato adventures that had Nogales traveling from the Afghan-Persian border to India to Singapore to Dutch-controlled Sumatra in modern Indonesia to the former Portuguese colony of Angola on the West African Coast to the former Union of South Africa to Argentina. All this done in a "helter skelter" sequence of adventures featuring an imprisoned Muslim emir, a

---

229 Nogales, *Looting of Nicaragua* (1928), pp. 217-18.
230 Nogales', *Memoirs of a Soldier of Fortune* (London (1931), p. 322 has the dramatized version of the salt tale not included in the London edition of *Looting of Nicaragua* (which lacks Chapters 12 and 13 of the New York edition of the book.))

human vampire, leopards, hyenas, elephants, and so on. As this supposedly occurred in "several months" in a "haphazard junket" made in 1900, when Nogales was aged twenty, we can understand where the initial skeptical comments about the book in the lengthy *Times of London* and *Spectator* reviews came from. It is also clear why Cunninghame Graham, whose public literary stature and sponsorship helped preserve Nogales' credibility, privately titled his friend's memoir the "Life and Miracles of General Nogales" when penning his long introduction on behalf of the book and its author.[231]

When *Memoirs* appeared in New York the next year, accordingly, all the aforementioned haphazard, abrupt, and disjointed globe-trotting adventures were gone. In their place was a far more restrained three pages stating that Nogales was publishing some portions of a life whose "one fixed specific purpose" was the liberation of his Venezuelan homeland from the tyranny oppressing it.[232]

What was a second chapter in the original London edition then became the main body of the first chapter in the later New York edition. Now, instead of frenetically globetrotting at age twenty, Nogales had returned to Venezuela after a thirteen year absence at age twenty. Unfortunately, Nogales' tales of his early life still had much of the miraculous about them. The "story-telling minstrel" part of Nogales' personality tried to mix with "military chief," and not always effectively.[233]

As Nogales told the new tale of returning to his homeland for the first time since being sent abroad by his parents at age seven, he was ridiculed for his German-accented Spanish by then-dictator Cipriano Castro in the presidential palace in Caracas in February of 1901.

---

231 Nogales, *Memoirs* (London, 1931), pp. 1-8, esp. 1, 5; Cunninghame Graham's handwritten preface is in the Robert Bontine Cunninghame Graham collection, Box 103, folder 2, in the National Library of Scotland Archives.
232 Nogales, *Memoirs* (New York, 1932), pp. 1-4, esp. 1-2.
233 ibid., p. 142.

Nogales quickly countered with negatives about Castro; and Castro ordered Nogales arrested for *lese majeste*. Fleeing to the Dominican Republic, Nogales quickly began plotting Castro's overthrow by getting supplies of money and guns from the president of Nicaragua after taking time out, en route, to try and assassinate the president of Guatemala. Back in the Dominican Republic awaiting the guns and money, a rebel chieftain from Nogales' native region ordered him to assist an attack against Castro's army that had begun on the Venezuelan-Colombian border. Leaving without the Nicaraguan aid, Nogales and thirty men, all Venezuelan exiles, sailed to the Goajira peninsula near the thinly settled entrance to Lake Maracaibo. There, a long, bloody battle ensued, during which Nogales was wounded by a bayonet thrust through the leg. Getting back to the boat he had hired with his few surviving companions through marauding Indian tribes, Nogales "set sail for Santo Domingo in quest of medical treatment and mental rest."[234]

Elements of this story may be true. A few of the people Nogales met are drawn three-dimensionally: an alcoholic American émigré, a Venezuelan exile traveling companion, an apolitical guide, a Haitian schooner owner. Others, however, appear and as suddenly disappear, without explanation. Dr. Carlos Rangel Garviras, for example, was described as a former Venezuelan president and "leader of the nationalist party of the Andean states" on whose orders Nogales went to fight against Castro in the first place. But after a single bloody and day-long give-no-quarter tropical battle which ended in a draw, and which Nogales later called a "disaster," Garviras completely drops out of the narrative, together with the general (named only Ortega) under whom Nogales fought. For the next eight years, Nogales stayed away from his homeland, only returning when Castro's dictatorship was overthrown by his lieutenant, Juan Vicente Gomez. No explanation for this gap is provided. Nor is it clear why Nogales initially

234 ibid, pp. 12-23.

supported Gomez in Caracas newspapers after he returned to Venezuela in 1909.[235]

Nogales' career as a liberator, therefore, was definitely episodic, so far as Venezuela was concerned. After the 1901 events, Nogales' overseas activity is then recorded as participation in a frenetic series of rebellions and gun-running episodes in the Caribbean and Central America, and military, rustling, and gold and silver mining adventures in China, Mexico, Alaska and Nevada.

The Chinese memoirs were most-clearly false. They involve claims of either military service or spying for the Japanese against the Russians in and around the Russian base at Port Arthur during the Russo-Japanese War of 1904-1905. The story was told only in the vaguest terms in a few sentences of the original London edition of *Memoirs*. The New York edition published the next year had a twenty-two page chapter featuring China's most-important politician (who else?) enrolling Nogales in espionage. Then the London edition of the sequel to *Memoirs*, published in 1934, told a completely different tale about what Nogales' Asian adventures had been, and when they had occurred.[236]

Nogales' webs of lies regarding the one trip he (may) have taken to Asia were the most dense because Asia was the most-segmented and distant news environment of all. Regarding his approximately six years in Alaska, Nevada, and on the Texas-Mexican border, however, Nogales seems to have fabricated a good deal less. It is necessary, however, to take most or all the famous Mexican revolution leaders he probably did not meet out of his narrative. It is also necessary to do the same with all the one-dimensional black-haired senoritas with flashing eyes that always joined Nogales in his adventures and all

235 Nogales, *Verdades...* (Caracas, 1910), p. 24 republishes a letter advocating voting for Gomez originally published in the newspaper *El Tiempo* in Caracas on October 9, 1909.
236 Nogales, *Memoirs* (London, 1931), p. 37; Nogales, *Memoirs* (New York, 1932), pp. 37-58; Nogales, *Silk Hat and Spurs*, (London (1934), pp. 151-61.

conveniently died while riding into glory or away from annihilation.
We are then left with a man who was a very competent rider, a
cowboy, and a cattle rustler along the Rio Grande. In Alaska and
Nevada, no famous politicians or beautiful women enter the narrative
at all. Nogales' life is one of survival against sometimes-major
environmental and human challenges on rugged sub-Arctic or desert
frontiers. Nogales survived, in particular, by knowing enough about
skills like surveying to record and mark-out mining claims; and was
socially respected because he was a very good man with a horse.[237]

When Nogales catches himself in lies in these North American
portions of *Memoirs of a Soldier of Fortune*, there is a curiously
gratuitous and unnecessary minstrelsy at work. During his years
prospecting and surveying in Alaska, for example, Nogales truthfully
said he visited an Inuit settlement near the mouth of the Yukon River
and on the coast of the Arctic Ocean. Missing ships headed south for
California in the fall of 1905, Nogales then claimed he got some Inuit
to take him over to Siberia in an ummiak, the only native craft that
had even the slightest chance of surviving some of the roughest
seasonal seas on Earth. Not content with this possible exaggeration,
Nogales followed it up with a complete fabrication. Not finding any
boat on the Russian side, Nogales said, he mushed (drove a team of
sled dogs) over the 90 miles of ice and water in the Bering Strait back
to Alaska near its narrowest point, while "crossing the [open water]
leads of the Straits in my sled which I turned into a sleigh boat by
wrapping its bottom with seal skins, sewed together and rendered
waterproof with walrus tallow."[238]

The author has spent enough time in Alaska to think this latter tale
was absurd. Helpful staff at the Alaska and Polar Regions Department
of the University of Alaska at Fairbanks put me in touch with
Professor Terence Cole of the Office of Public History at the
University. "Of course," he observed, "the Siberia mushing story is

---

237 Nogales, *Memoirs* (New York, 1932), pp. 50-158.
238 ibid., p. 90.

just hooey [a refreshingly non-academic word for nonsense]." No possible way existed for Nogales to have done what he claimed to have done crossing the Bering Strait. The statement about turning his sled into a boat is as ridiculous as saying he transformed his canoe into an airplane.[239]

What Professor Cole went on to term Nogales "talent for expansion", however, was hardly unique to him. At exactly the same time as Nogales' book appeared, the English edition of Jan Welzl's *Thirty Years in the Golden North* appeared; with a glowing introduction by noted Czech author Karel Capek (who, among many other things, invented the word "robot."). Welzl's exercise in utter fantasy arrayed as truth was published by a very reputable British-based house and was widely reviewed in both Europe and America. It was based on the concept that a Czech sailor achieved princely greatness among peoples and places of the Russian, U.S. and Canadian Arctic. Welzl's thorough inventions made Nogales' lies look like those of a devout choirboy in comparison. Both kinds of falsehoods – complete and partial – were possible in an era of segmented news environments when even western Europe was seven to ten days distance from New York City, and when making a now-simple telephone call to London from New York cost over fifty of today's dollars, if you had reserved a line with a human operator the day before. Given, additionally, that travel from even settled points in Alaska to New York City could easily take two weeks, and that only small minorities of the affluent, the devout, or immigrants in search of political asylum or a better life ever took such lengthy trips at all, good story-tellers could weave "Orientalist" or other fables about unfamiliar lands and cultures with very little fear of exposure.[240]

Truths and Fictions

After 1934, then, the focus of Nogales' life shifted away from fact and towards fantasy, and from publishing to Hollywood. As *Memoirs*

239 Professor Terrence Cole to author, e-mail dated January 3, 2007.

appeared in a French translation and ran serially in a German newspaper, Nogales wrote his friend Cunninghame Graham that "here the yarn has run out on me, since I find myself with nothing more to say." An often-frustrated man of action, Nogales spent several months in and around Los Angeles looking to interest a Hollywood studio in purchasing movie rights to either *Memoirs* or its sequel, *Silk Hat and Spurs*, which had just appeared in London.[241]

None of these efforts was successful. Sponsors like Cunninghame Graham and Lowell Thomas helped save *Memoirs* and to make it Nogales' most successful book. His luck ran out with *Silk Hat and Spurs*, however, and he had only himself to blame. Despite a glowing introduction from Viscount Allenby, Field Marshal and victorious commander of all British, allied, and Imperial forces in Syria and Palestine in World War I. Nogales returned to the staccato series of globetrotting stories that marred the original London edition of *Memoirs*. Straight-off, the book began with fantasy women alternating with illusory youthful commissions in the Spanish and Moroccan armies. And on it went. There was truth in the book, including portions of a trip across the then utterly undeveloped Mexican state of Quintana Roo in the Yucatan and – as always – Nogales' very real experiences in the Ottoman Army and traveling

---

240 For Jan Welzl, see the English translation of his *Thirty Tears in the Golden North* (with a Foreword by Karel Capek), (New York, Macmillan, 1932). Welzl's *The Quest for Polar Treasures* appeared with Macmillan the next year. For the continuing force of fantasies such as lost Indian cities and cultures in the Amazon, see, i.e., Brian Fawcett (ed.), *Lost Trails, Lost Cities, By Colonel P. H. Fawcett* (New York, Funk and Wagnall's, 1953). Fawcett disappeared in the Amazon in 1925. See also David Grann, *The Lost City of Z: A Tale of Deadly Obsession in the Amazon* (Garden City, Doubleday, 2009), which is the latest biography of Fawcett.

241 Nogales to Cunninghame Graham, July 19, 1933, Cunninghame Graham Papers, National Library of Scotland Archives; Lee Shippey, "The Lee Side o' L.A.", *Los Angeles Times*, August 14, 1934, p. A-4. See also other *Los Angeles Times* descriptions of dinners and meetings Nogales attended in the issues of August 7, 1934 (page A-8); October 18, 1934 (page A-24), and November 8, 1934 (page A-6).

along the Venezuelan-Colombian border regions where he had been born fifty-five years before.[242]

This time, however, Nogales' fourth and final book was not reviewed anywhere. His literary agent and editor Constance Murray Skinner and he had somehow parted company at some time in 1929 or 1930. Cunninghame Graham was now in his early 80s and very frail. Lowell Thomas and Muna Lee were helping to forward (or create) the reputations of other people. Luis Munoz Marin was well on the way to moderating his politics and becoming the "Father of Puerto Rico". Rafael De Nogales, meanwhile, struck a columnist who met him in Los Angeles as "a little, wiry nervous man whose life has been so filled with astonishing adventures that it is hard for him to tell a connected story of any of them."[243]

There was quiet tragedy here. Nogales was part of some of the most important political events of his age. He knew war, genocide, revolution, and the rise of the oil age (and petroleum-based dictatorships) as few writers of his time did. His misfortune was to operate in portions of the globe about which most American intellectuals knew little and cared to know no more. The Middle East (then) and Latin America and the Caribbean (still) are regions where expertise, such as it is, tends to exist in fits and starts. Until 9/11, "Arabs" did not have to be taken very seriously except when petroleum prices were an issue. Many policymakers who understood Arabic and wider regional issues were a tiny elite whose roots stretched all the way back to a tiny number of English-speaking missionary families operating in the Middle East in the late 19th and early 20th centuries – or to the somewhat more numerous harder-eyed and looser-living U.S. oil executives who followed them after World War II. Turkey is still marginal except as a regional military

---

242 Nogales, *Silk Hat and Spurs*, pp. 16-21, i.e.; The Turkish Army memoirs begin on page 223.
243 Lee Shippey, "The Lee Side o' L.A.," *Los Angeles Times*, August 14, 1934, p. A-4.

peacekeeper. Latin Americans, meanwhile, are still waiting for much in the way of U.S. diplomatic expertise or sustained attention. For them, as one Latin joke has it, it is always Monday morning.[244]

Conclusion: Death in a Minor Key

As the shadows of Nogales' life lengthened around him he remembered, as aging men do, images and events of a past now lost. His pride in his service as a regular Ottoman army officer steadily increased. Now, Nogales had been part of a Turkish army putting down an "Armenian revolution" in Eastern Anatolia and one not involved in Armenian massacres elsewhere. Nogales' cross-cultural identification was complete enough that he used phrases like "... we Turks knew how to handle that Arab rabble and keep them in their proper place" or, "we Turks" won the First and Second Battles of Gaza. He also described his arrival in Aleppo, Syria after six months with Turkish forces in Anatolia as a reintroduction to Western folkways.

"(W)hen I... saw the first Europeans parading through the streets sporting stiff collars, neckties, and umbrellas, I frankly had to laugh, almost as much as if I had seen the bearded lady, the skeleton man or some other freak of a dime museum running amok through the streets of New York."[245]

A major reason that Nogales so well remembered his Ottoman military service, and so thoroughly bonded with and respected his men and his fellow officers, was that he had more power, prestige, legitimacy and rank in a Turkish empire than he had ever had at any other point in his life. As a captain – and, later, major – of cavalry, Rafael De Nogales became the soldier-scholar of his hopes and dreams.

---

244 Robert D. Kaplan. *The Arabists: The Romance of an American Elite* (New York, Free Press, 1995), covers Syria, Lebanon and Saudi Arabia, but not Egypt or Turkey.
245 Nogales, *Silk Hat and Spurs*, pp. 238, 223, 279.

Compared to T. E. Lawrence, Nogales was anything but an introspective or ideology-driven man. He also lacked many of those elliptical and hidden habits of mind that led some of Lawrence's friends to observe that his personal motto should be: "Incognito, Ergo Sum," (I am disguised, therefore I am). The military memoir and narrative that Nogales told, however, had complexities and truths that the versions of Lawrence's career made available commercially during his lifetime and by his friends immediately after his death did not. Nogales' Turks, Nicaraguans, or Venezuelans were not Lawrence's Bedouins; brave unspoiled primitives fighting a just war of liberation. Instead, they were soldiers, politicians, peasants, and officials facing civil conflicts on top of foreign invasions. At issue was whether their fledgling nationalisms would survive at all. Nogales did not present himself as a conquering imperial hero whose statements about himself mixed the romantic, the dramatic, the enigmatic, and the equivocal. Instead, when dealing with the realities, as opposed to the later contrived illusions of his career, he "savored his pitfalls as thoroughly as his triumphs" and referred to himself as "the humble acolyte of an unripe god."[246]

Nogales' world, then, was one of far more political and moral ambiguity than Lawrence's. Those most brave and heroic froze to death in Caucasian mountain passes or died at their posts after repeated massive attacks. Political soldiers unjustly "borrowed" fame earned by professional soldiers. Men were not by nature noble. Victims were also victimizers. Had the roles of Armenians and Turks been reversed in 1915, Anatolia would not have lacked for innocent dead, or mass expulsions of innocents to create the Greater Armenia of Armenian nationalists like Dr. Karekin Basdermadjian (Armen Garo's) dreams. In Nogales' world, often-unknown peoples did what they had to do to survive, empires were often brutal fights for resources and regional dominance, racisms were thorough, and the

---

246 Knightley and Simpson, op. cit, p. x; R. Norris Blake, op. cit., p. 550; Nogales, *Soldier of Fortune* (New York, 1932), p. 243.

certainties of the Pax Britannica in and around the Middle East or the developing Pax Americana in the Caribbean and Central America were anything but commonplace. In Nogales' world, some Armenians did rebel (Armen Garo). This led to regional murders and massacres (Cevdet Bey in Van) that became an empire-wide policy by a "process of cumulative policy radicalization" (Interior Minister Talat Pasha, the "Special Organization," and the Social Darwinian wing of the Young Turks). Finally, the Ottoman Empire's economic and organizational inabilities to care for the hundreds of thousands not killed but expelled from their villages completed an already grim picture.[247]

Nogales, then, was very aware of what most Britons or Americans of his time did *not* know about the lands to which he travelled. Because he was used to operating at the intersection of cultures and had the linguistic facility to do-so, Nogales also understood the sometimes-explosive mix of ethnicities and religious differences that the past had bequeathed to the present. These, the dominant influence of geography, the push for resources, and emergent nationalisms were largely what Nogales' conceptual world was all about.

---

247 My argument, here, follows Donald Bloxham, *The Great Game of Genocide: Imperialism, Nationalism, and the Destruction of the Ottoman Armenians* (New York, Oxford University Press, 2007), i.e., pp 69ff and Michael Mann, *The Dark Side of Democracy: Explaining Ethnic Cleansing* (New York, Cambridge University Press, 2005), pp. 111-73. For the size of the restored Armenia that Armenian nationalists wanted, as of 1918, see the map at the rear of Dr. Gregorin Pasdermadjian, *Why Armenia Should Be Free; Armenia's Role in the Present War* (Boston, Hairenik Publishing Company, 1918). The extent of land is considerably greater than that of historic Armenia as recorded in Razmik Panossian, *The Armenians: From Kings and Priests to Merchants and Traders* (New York, Columbia University Press, 2006), p. xviii. Pasdermadjian's claims include, for example, "Cilician Armenia" on the Mediterranean that Panossian dates to only between the 11th and 14th centuries. For a pathbreaking discussion between Turkish and Armenian scholars see the special issue of *Armenian Forum* 1, no. 2 (Princeton, 1998).

The homeland he loved, however, benefitted little from Nogales' knowledge, or his life. An inconsistent rebel and longtime exile and outsider, Nogales was never able to cooperate with other opponents of Juan Vicente Gomez – with the single and important exception of Luis Munoz Marin of Puerto Rico during his pan-American socialism phase in the 1920s. Born in an era of *caudillismo* by regional military strongmen, Nogales never

Juan Vicente Gomez in later life

quite got beyond the concept that the way to change a society was to form a militia, issue a pronunciamento, march on the capital, and order change accomplished from the top down. The exile experience of the students of the Generation of 1928, however, accustomed them to a different, popular, and organization-centered approach to modernization and social change. Bolshevik Russia was a model for some of those young Latin Americans; democratic socialism was a model for others. Still more had experience with catholic social action movements or with a Mexican Revolution which had gone from caudillismo to a popular front and party-based political structure from 1910 to the late 1920s.[248]

---

248 John D. Martz, op. cit, pp. 20-27; De Trinca, op. cit, pp. 105-17; Hellinger, op. cit., pp. 46 51.

These generation-based political differences became particularly important when on December 15, 1935, the first rumors surfaced in Caracas that dictator Juan Vicente Gomez had died. Revenge was swift. Local government officials, landowners, spies, family members, and "hombrecitos" were punished by those they had wronged. Because the armed forces and a varied collection of domestic and foreign opposition groups initially cooperated to insure no Gomez follower could seize leadership, the end of what the *Washington Post* rightly called "one of the longest and strongest dictatorships of modern times" came by mid-January, 1936.[249]

At this point, prisons started being opened and exiles started coming home. Nogales, in exile for twenty-five years, told the Associated Press, as reported in the *Washington Post*, that "his chief function in Venezuela would be to reorganize the army and make of it a police force."[250]

Whatever a united front of Venezuelan exiles informally or otherwise decided in January, conditions on the ground in Venezuela were far more complicated. Venezuelan army commander General Eleazar Lopez Contreras stood aside while many of Gomez's family and henchmen fled; and many of those that didn't flee were killed. Gomez's cabinet officers, meanwhile, chose General Contreras as president. Unions and political parties were cautiously allowed. Venezuela, however, was anything but a democracy. Suffrage was restricted to the literate in a mostly unschooled and illiterate country. Elections were indirect, not direct. Those who had long profited under "El Benemerito's" system of "crony capitalism" had no desire to change the basics of the system; while the two percent of the labor force newly organized into petroleum workers unions had no desire to maintain it. A general strike in Caracas in February of 1936 was

---

249 Rourke, op. cit, pp. 286-300; "Venezuela Sees Its Democracy Reviving," *Washington Post*, January 12, 1936, p. B-10.
250 "Venezuela Sees Its Democracy Reviving," *Washington Post*, January 12, 1936, p. B-10. (Nogales' first name was misspelled as Raphael in the story.

met with swift military and police repression. A new wave of riots followed to liquidate Gomez' allies. The military warned of communist subversions.[251]

In such a situation, about the last thing that General Lopez Contreras intended to do was to reorganize the Venezuelan army, under the direction of Rafael De Nogales or anyone else. Nogales, therefore, became a returned exile without a job. He waited in a hotel room in Caracas for four months without result, except to chat and reminisce with occasional young Venezuelan military officers who stopped in to see him. Lopez Contreras, decently, gave Nogales enough for the first small printing of his memoir

General Eleazar Lopez Contreras

Four Years in his own country – the small earnings from which paid Nogales' living expenses. Finally, in May of 1936, Nogales was offered a relatively minor job to get him out of the capital. He became the customs' administrator for a minor port near Lake Maracaibo in western Venezuela, where U.S. oil tankers loaded Venezuelan crude from a pipeline. Boredom, alcohol, and official expectations that he would finance much of his salary via petty corruption made Nogales leave the job after about four months. Back in Caracas after October

251　Rourke, op. cit, pp. 300-10; Hellinger, op. cit, pp. 59-60.

of 1936, he was a Venezuelan relatively well-known abroad, but almost with no standing at home.[252]

Nogales' state of limbo continued as General (and President) Lopez Contreras tightened the screws on the political opposition and the new unions. By March of 1937, he expelled forty-seven opposition leaders from Venezuela. Others he tried to expel, like Romulo Betancourt, went into hiding. Not until 10 years after Gomez's death did a stable and peaceful transition from dictatorship to democracy start taking root in a country where peaceful transitions of power were almost unknown.[253]

Nogales, meanwhile, remained an awkward guest. Enough so that Lopez Contreras' Interior Minister finally gave him a job befitting his interests. Keeping him away from the Venezuelan military, where he had more combat experience than many senior officers, Nogales was to go abroad and study the "National Guard" or "Civil Guard" systems in Panama, Cuba, the United States, Germany, Italy and Great Britain. Nogales understood the importance of these militia adjuncts to regular armies. He had, after all, begun his military service in the Ottoman army with the Regiment of the Gendarmes of Van in Anatolia 23 years before.[254]

In July of 1937, after eighteen months of frustration, then, Rafael De Nogales set off on his mission. But, like T. E. Lawrence's demise following a motorcycle accident in May, 1935 shortly after retiring from the R.A.F., Nogales' was to be a death in a minor key. Coming down with a throat infection in Panama, on the first stage of his journey, Nogales was operated on. Then, in a pre-antibiotics era, his infection worsened, and he died in hospital there on July 10, 1937, aged fifty-seven.[255]

---

252 De Trinca, p. 89, Nweheid, op. cit., pp. 162-63; R. Norris Blake, op. cit., p. 551 reports over-use of alcohol at this point in Nogales' career.

253 John D. Martz, op. cit, pp. 31-32; Romulo Betancourt, op. cit, pp. 56-59.

254 De Trinca, op cit., pp. 87-92; Nweheid, op. cit, p. 163.

255 Nweheid, p. 163; De Trinca, p. 92.

T. E. Lawrence had been lauded after his sudden death at age forty-six in 1935. Editorials and eminences hailed him as one of the finest and most patriotic Englishmen of his time, whose every act was one of a gallant celebrity. He was memorialized with the greats of English politics and empire in St. Paul's Cathedral in London, and buried in a tomb befitting a medieval Crusader. All the negatives of his life from illegitimacy to overstatement to his sometimes-bizarre approaches to sexuality were scrupulously ignored. In all the years since Lawrence's *Seven Pillars of Wisdom* first became commercially available following his death, the book has never been out of print in English.[256]

Rafael De Nogales, meanwhile, died largely unknown. Lacking surviving family in Venezuela, he would not even have been buried but for the generosity of pilot Jesus R. Blanco, whom he had met during his trip to Nicaragua in 1927 and who helped him during his final months in Caracas. Blanco opened part of his own family's plot to Nogales' remains, where they stayed until 1975 – after which Nogales was honorably interred in a cemetery for Venezuelan military officers.[257]

As Nogales was first buried, late in 1937, Argentinean author Roberto Arlt queried why Lawrence was remembered and Nogales forgotten. Both were gentleman adventurers and authors. Both had blood on their hands. Both understood media and self-promotion, and used it successfully. Both, additionally, were loners who generally operated without close or long-term friendships. Why was one deemed to be a paragon of his times and his culture, and the other a footnote? Latin America's remaining on the sidelines in both of the world wars of the twentieth century that shook Europe, Asia, Africa, and the Middle East provides part of the answer. So do individual

---

256 For the Lawrence cult, see Crawford, op. cit., and Brown (2004), pp. 188-89 (for *Seven Pillars of Wisdom*, publication status from 1935-2005).

257 De Trinca, pp. 93-94; Nweheid, op. cit, pp. 163.

characteristics like Nogales' megalomania. Lawrence, meanwhile, fought to preserve and expand the power of a fading empire. He succeeded, and is enshrined among the last generation of such successful imperial heroes. Nogales' older empire went down in defeat, to then be succeeded by a collection of often contending ethnic, national, and religious movements. Nogales knew, as Lawrence did not, that there could be a very dark side indeed to fledgling nationalisms, if the circumstances were right. As one result, Nogales early despised Nazi leader Adolf Hitler and all he represented. Lawrence's career is generally presented as a triumph of a man who found his heroic moment in history. Nogales' career is one of survival, not heroism, and of moral ambiguity, not attainment or ascendancy. Lawrence's world was one of British legal and cultural superiority. Nogales's global view was of many rule-sets simultaneously contending for dominance, and of power politics, in the end, being an amoral business based upon control of strategic geography and resources. Lawrence's world was one of European and English-speaking ascendancy. Nogales' world was one of survival of the conquered and emergent Asian powers. Lawrence embodies success. Rafael De Nogales, a trimly built, nervous, emotional, biracial, multicultural and high-strung Latin American very proud of his country and his nation, reminds us that losers can often have as important historical lessons to teach as do winners.[258, 259]

---

258   Roberto Arlt, "Lawrence, 500,000 dolares? Y Rafael de Nogales?," *El Mundo* (Buenos Aires), November 15, 1937, reprinted as "Vidas Paralelas" in Arlt, *Aguafuertes gallegas y asturianas* (Buenos Aires, Losada, 1999); Earl Parker Hanson, op. cit., p. 105 (for Nogales hating Hitler "venomously".); *San Francisco Chronicle Sunday Magazine*, September 11, 1927 (for characterization of Nogales). For Lawrence and British fascists in 1934, see Wilson, op. cit., pp. 916-918.

259 There are also important points of literacy cultural narrative to be made here. My associate, Spanish teacher Jaime Pavlish, has noticed parallels between the stories of Nogales and Miguel Cervantes and his eternal character and alter ego Don Quijote and, to a lesser extent, to Lawrence as well. All three of them, Quijote, Lawrence and Nogales had a grand messianic sense of mission that was often misunderstood and even mocked by others. All three, Nogales, Lawrence, and Cervantes/Quijote lived the medieval ideal of being men of both arms and letters. All three had extensive interactions with the Turks and Islam, but of course only Nogales actually fought on the side of the Turks. All three died relatively disillusioned and under obscure circumstances. All three had doubtful ancestry. Lawrence was illegitimate, Nogales changed his name and was possibly illegitimate, Cervantes was probably of Jewish converse background; and of course Don Quijote's origins are purposely obscured by Cervantes. Nogales, like Cervantes, was an adventurer and combat veteran who then sought to earn money through his writings after the fighting was over. Lawrence, meanwhile, preferred fame to money and achieved it – with the not-insubstantial help of American publicist Lowell Thomas. Don Quijote is forever obsessing about the chivalric code of the knight errant and his role in righting wrongs. Nogales and Lawrence were no strangers to the chivalric code, though perhaps more often in the breach than in the observances. Lawrence censored himself to preserve imperial properties. Nogales, like Cervantes, wrote in fear of the censor and was translated into several languages, with the English edition of his major work the most popular. This recalls the literary device that Cervantes used when he claimed Don Quijote was a translation from Cid Hamete's mysterious manuscript in Arabic. In spite of all these similarities, how can one take seriously a comparison of two flesh and blood individuals with a character in a book? Here it pays to remember the enduring strength of cultural role-models, including King Arthur and Sir Lancelot. Many commentators have observed that the figure of Don Quijote is more real than most actual individuals that have ever lived. More than all this, however, is the primal nature of the story of Don Quijote that reverberates throughout Spanish and, indeed, world literature up to the present day. See, for example, *Selected Works of Miguel de Unamuno*, trans. Anthony Kerrigan, (Princeton: Princeton University Press, 1967).

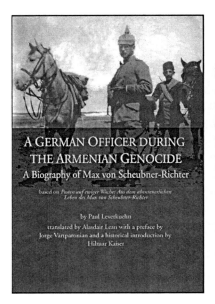

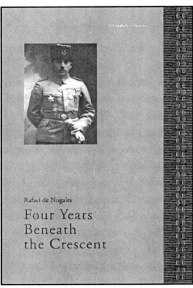

Gomidas Institute Imprints

Rafael Nogales, *Four Years Beneath the Crescent*, (London: Sterndale Classics), 2003.

Harry Sturmer, *Two War Years in Constantinople: Sketches of German and Young Turkish Ethics and Politics,* (London: Sterndale Classics), 2005.

Paul Leverkuehn, *A German Officer during the Armenian Genocide: A Biography of Max Scheubner-Richter,* (London: Gomidas Institute), 2009.

Contact: *info@gomidas.org*

LaVergne, TN USA
03 May 2010

181351LV00004B/39/P